I0411475

Temperate Interior West Community Tree Guide:
Benefits, Costs, and Strategic Planting

Kelaine E. Vargas, E. Gregory McPherson, James R. Simpson, Paula J. Peper, Shelley L. Gardner, and Qingfu Xiao

U.S. Department of Agriculture, Forest Service
Pacific Southwest Research Station
Albany, CA

General Technical Report
PSW-GTR-206
November 2007

This work was sponsored by the U.S. Department of Agriculture, Forest Service, State and Private Forestry, Urban and Community Forestry Program; the State of Nevada, Department of Conservation and Natural Resources, Division of Forestry; the State of Idaho, Department of Lands, Community Forestry; and the City of Boise, Department of Parks and Recreation.

Abstract

Vargas, Kelaine E.; McPherson, E. Gregory; Simpson, James R.; Peper, Paula J.; Gardner, Shelley L.; Xiao, Qingfu. 2007. Temperate Interior West community tree guide: benefits, costs, and strategic planting. Gen. Tech. Rep. PSW-GTR-206. Albany, CA: U.S. Department of Agriculture, Forest Service, Pacific Southwest Research Station. 108 p.

Even as they increase the beauty of our surroundings, trees provide us with a great many ecosystem services, including air quality improvement, energy conservation, stormwater interception, and atmospheric carbon dioxide reduction. These benefits must be weighed against the costs of maintaining trees, including planting, pruning, irrigation, administration, pest control, liability, cleanup, and removal. We present benefits and costs for representative small, medium, and large deciduous trees and coniferous trees in the Temperate Interior West region derived from models based on indepth research carried out in Boise, Idaho. Average annual net benefits increase with tree size and differ based on location: $12 (public) to $24 (yard) for a small tree, $30 (public) to $45 (yard) for a medium tree, $49 (public) to $63 (yard) for a large tree, $22 (public) to $25 (yard) for a conifer. Two hypothetical examples of planting projects are described to illustrate how the data in this guide can be adapted to local uses, and guidelines for maximizing benefits and reducing costs are given.

Keywords: Ecosystem services, Temperate Interior West, urban forestry, benefit-cost analysis.

Executive Summary

This report quantifies benefits and costs for representative small, medium, and large deciduous trees and conifers in the Temperate Interior West region: the species chosen as representative are the crabapple, Norway maple, white ash, and blue spruce (see "Common and Scientific Names" section). The analysis describes "yard trees" (those planted in residential sites) and "public trees" (those planted on streets or in parks). Benefits are calculated based on tree growth curves and numerical models that consider regional climate, building characteristics, air pollutant concentrations, and prices. Tree care costs and mortality rates are based on results from a survey of municipal and commercial arborists. We assume a 43-percent survival rate over a 40-year timeframe.

The measurements used in modeling environmental and other benefits of trees are based on indepth research carried out in Boise, Idaho. Given the Temperate Interior West region's diverse geographical area, this approach provides general approximations based on some necessary assumptions that serve as a starting point for more specific local calculations. It is a general accounting that can be easily adapted and adjusted for local planting projects. Two examples are provided that illustrate how to adjust benefits and costs to reflect different aspects of local urban forest improvement projects.

Large trees provide the most benefits. Average annual benefits increase with mature tree size and differ based on tree location. The lowest values are for yard trees on the southern side of houses, and the highest values are for yard trees on the western side of houses. Values for public trees are intermediate. Average annual benefits range as follows:

- $25 to $32 for a small tree

- $39 to $55 for a medium tree

- $58 to $74 for a large tree

- $32 to $33 for a conifer

Benefits associated with reduced energy use and increased aesthetic and other benefits reflected in higher property values account for the largest proportion of total benefits in this region. Reduced levels of stormwater runoff, air pollutants, and carbon dioxide (CO_2) in the air are the next most important benefits.

Energy conservation benefits differ with tree location as well as size. Trees located opposite west-facing walls provide the greatest net heating and cooling energy savings. Reducing heating and cooling energy needs reduces CO_2 emissions and thereby reduces atmospheric CO_2. Similarly, energy savings that reduce

Benefits and costs quantified

Average annual benefits

Costs

demand from power plants account for important reductions in gases that produce ozone, a major component of smog, and other air pollutants.

The benefits of trees are offset by the costs of caring for them. Based on our surveys of municipal and residential arborists, the average annual cost for tree care ranges from $7 to $19 per tree. (Values below are for yard and public trees, respectively.)

- $8 and $16 for a small tree
- $10 and $18 for a medium tree
- $11 and $19 for a large tree
- $7 and $12 for a conifer

Planting costs, annualized over 40 years, are a significant expense ($4 per tree per year). Pruning ($1 to $7 per tree per year) and removal and disposal annualized over 40 years ($2 to $3 per tree per year) are the next greatest costs. Public trees also incur administrative expense ($2 to $3 per tree per year). During the establishment period, costs for labor-intensive hand watering were estimated to be $2 per year for 5 years.

Average annual net benefits

Average annual net benefits (benefits minus costs) per tree for a 40-year period differ with tree location and tree size and range from a low of $12 to a high of $62 per tree.

- $12 for a small public tree to $24 for a small yard tree on the west side of a house
- $29 for a medium yard tree on the south side of a house to $45 for a medium yard tree on the west side of a house
- $47 for a large yard tree on the south side of a house to $63 for a large yard tree on the west side of a house
- $22 for a public conifer to $25 for a yard conifer in a windbreak

Environmental benefits alone, including energy savings, stormwater runoff reduction, improved air quality, and reduced atmospheric CO_2, can be more than five times tree care costs.

Net benefits summed over 40 years

Net benefits for a yard tree opposite a west wall and a public tree are substantial when summed over the 40-year period (values below are for yard trees opposite a west wall and public trees, respectively):

- $953 and $479 for a small tree
- $1,784 and $1,184 for a medium tree

- $2,497 and $1,931 for a large tree

- $984 and $840 for a conifer

Yard trees produce higher net benefits than public trees, primarily because of lower maintenance costs.

To demonstrate ways that communities can adapt the information in this report to their needs, examples of two fictional cities interested in improving their urban forest have been created. The benefits and costs of different planting projects are determined. In the hypothetical city of Chinook Valley, net benefits and benefit-cost ratios (BCRs; total benefits divided by costs) are calculated for a planting of 1,000 trees (2-in caliper) assuming a cost of $200 per tree, 43 percent mortality rate, and 40-year analysis. Total benefits are $2.16 million, total costs are about $750,000, and net benefits are $1.41 million ($35.73 per tree per year). The BCR is 2.93:1, indicating that $2.93 is returned for every $1 invested. The net benefits and BCRs (in parentheses) by mature tree size are:

- $16,396 (1.49:1) for 50 crabapple trees

- $149,988 (2.33:1) for 150 Norway maples

- $1,185,384 (3.19:1) for 700 white ash

- $73,801 (2.48:1) for 100 blue spruce

Increased property values reflecting aesthetic and other benefits of trees account for about half (46 percent) of the estimated benefits, and reduced energy costs for another 40 percent. Reduced stormwater runoff (10 percent), air quality improvement (2 percent), and atmospheric CO_2 reduction (2 percent) make up the remaining benefits.

In the fictional city of Solanum, long-term planting and tree care costs and benefits were compared to determine if a proposed policy that might favor planting small trees would be cost-effective compared to the current policy of planting large trees where space permits. Over a 40-year period, the net benefits are:

- $385 for a small tree

- $1,070 for a medium tree

- $1,791 for a large tree

Based on this analysis, the city of Solanum decided to strengthen its tree ordinance, requiring developers to create tree shade plans that show how they will achieve 50-percent shade over streets, sidewalks, and parking lots within 15 years of development.

Contents

1   **Chapter 1. Introduction**

1   **The Temperate Interior West Region**

5   **Chapter 2. Benefits and Costs of Urban and Community Forests**

5   **Benefits**

5   Saving Energy

8   Reducing Atmospheric Carbon Dioxide

10   Improving Air Quality

13   Reducing Stormwater Runoff and Improving Hydrology

16   Aesthetics and Other Benefits

20   **Costs**

21   Planting and Maintaining Trees

22   Conflicts With Urban Infrastructure

25   **Chapter 3. Benefits and Costs of Community Forests in Temperate Interior West Communities**

25   **Overview of Procedures**

25   Approach

29   Reporting Results

29   **Findings of This Study**

29   Average Annual Net Benefits

30   Average Annual Costs

32   Average Annual Benefits

37   **Chapter 4. Estimating Benefits and Costs for Tree Planting Projects in Your Community**

37   **Applying Benefit-Cost Data**

37   Chinook Valley Example

42   City of Solanum Example

45   **Increasing Program Cost-Effectiveness**

45   Increasing Benefits

46   Reducing Program Costs

49 **Chapter 5. General Guidelines for Selecting and Placing Trees**

49 **Guidelines for Energy Savings**

49 Maximizing Energy Savings from Shading

51 Planting Windbreaks for Heating Savings

52 Selecting Trees to Maximize Benefits

53 **Guidelines for Reducing Carbon Dioxide**

54 **Guidelines for Reducing Stormwater Runoff**

55 **Guidelines for Improving Air Quality Benefits**

56 **Guidelines for Avoiding Conflicts With Infrastructure**

58 **Guidelines for Maximizing Long-Term Benefits**

61 **Glossary of Terms**

66 **Common and Scientific Names**

67 **Metric Equivalents**

67 **Acknowledgments**

68 **References**

81 **Appendix 1: Additional Resources**

83 **Appendix 2: Benefit–Cost Information Tables**

93 **Appendix 3: Procedures for Estimating Benefits and Costs**

93 **Approach**

93 Pricing Benefits and Costs

93 Growth Modeling

95 Reporting Results

96 Benefit and Cost Valuation

96 **Calculating Benefits**

96 Calculating Energy Benefits

98 Atmospheric Carbon Dioxide Reduction

101 Stormwater Benefits

102 Aesthetic and Other Benefits

104 **Calculating Costs**

104 Planting

104   Pruning

105   Tree and Stump Removal

105   Pest and Disease Control

105   Irrigation Costs

105   Other Costs for Public and Yard Trees

106   **Calculating Net Benefits**

106   Benefits Accrue at Different Scales

108   **Limitations of This Study**

Chapter 1. Introduction

The Temperate Interior West Region

From Boise, Idaho, to Reno, Nevada, to the cities of southeastern Washington and some parts of coastal Oregon, and portions of southern California, the Temperate Interior West region (fig. 1) contains a diverse assemblage of municipalities. The **climate**[1] of this region, which corresponds to Sunset climate zone 3 (Brenzel 2001), is characterized by hot, dry summers and winters that are cold but milder than the surrounding areas. Average summer high temperatures range from the low 90s in the interior areas to the high 60s along the Oregon coast; winter low temperatures in the interior regions are usually below freezing and may drop far below zero, whereas winters along the coast are much milder, with low temperatures averaging in the mid to upper 30s. Precipitation rates range from approximately 30 in along the Oregon coast to 8 in Reno, with the majority falling in the winter.

Scope of the Temperate Interior West region

Figure 1—The Temperate Interior West region covers the milder areas of the snowy West, including eastern areas of the Columbia River, portions of Nevada east of the Sierra Nevada, portions of southern California, and the coast ranges of Oregon and Washington.

---

[1] Words in bold are defined in the glossary.

Temperate Interior West communities can derive many benefits from urban forests

As the communities of the Temperate Interior West continue to grow and change during the coming decades, growing and sustaining healthy **community forests** is integral to the quality of life that residents experience. The urban forest is a distinctive feature of the landscape that protects us from the elements, cleans the water we drink and the air we breathe, and forms a connection to earlier generations who planted and tended the trees.

The role of urban forests in enhancing the environment, increasing community attractiveness and livability, and fostering civic pride takes on greater significance as communities strive to balance economic growth with environmental quality and social well-being. The simple act of planting trees provides opportunities to connect residents with nature and with each other (fig. 2). Neighborhood tree plantings and stewardship projects stimulate investment by local citizens, businesses, and governments for the betterment of their communities. Community forests bring opportunity for economic renewal, combating development woes, and increasing the quality of life for community residents.

Temperate Interior West communities can promote energy efficiency through tree planting and stewardship programs that strategically locate trees to save energy and minimize conflicts with urban infrastructure. The same trees can provide additional benefits by reducing stormwater runoff; improving local air, soil, and water quality; reducing atmospheric carbon dioxide (CO_2); providing wildlife habitat; increasing property values; slowing traffic; enhancing community attractiveness and investment; and promoting human well-being.

Figure 2—Tree planting and stewardship programs provide opportunities for local residents to work together to build better communities.

Although trees can provide many benefits to residents of the Temperate Interior West, trees are not always an inherent part of these ecosystems. Therefore few native species may be available for planting, and those that are may be inappropriate for urban settings. There may be concern over the introduction of nonnative trees that they may prove to be invasive, particularly in riparian areas, provide habitat for nonnative fauna, and encroach on nearby native habitats. These concerns are valid, considering for example, the invasion of the tree of heaven (see "Common and Scientific Names" section) along the Sacramento and American Rivers in California (Hunter 2000) and along the Rio Grande (Tellman 1997) and of Russian olive throughout the Western United States (Brock 1998). Careful species selection in collaboration with your local extension agent or city forester can allay these concerns while allowing local communities to reap the many benefits of trees in urban areas.

This guide builds upon studies by the USDA Forest Service in Chicago and Sacramento (McPherson et al. 1994, 1997), and other regional tree guides from the Center for Urban Forest Research (McPherson et al. 1999b, 2000, 2003, 2004, 2006a, 2006b, 2006c, in press; Vargas et al., in press) to extend knowledge of urban forest benefits in the Temperate Interior West. The guide:

Scope defined

- Quantifies benefits of trees on a per-tree basis rather than on a canopy cover basis (it should not be used to estimate benefits for trees growing in forest stands).

- Describes management costs and benefits.

- Details how tree planting programs can improve environmental quality, conserve energy, and add value to communities.

- Explains where to place residential yard and public trees to maximize their benefits and cost-effectiveness.

- Describes ways to minimize conflicts between trees and power lines, sidewalks, and buildings.

- Illustrates how to use this information to estimate benefits and costs for local tree planting projects.

These guidelines are specific to the Temperate Interior West, and are based on data and calculations from open-growing urban trees in this region.

Street, park, and shade trees are components of all Temperate Interior West communities, and they affect every resident. Their benefits are myriad. However, with municipal tree programs dependent on taxpayer-supported general funds, communities are forced to ask whether trees are worth the price to plant and care for over the long term, thus requiring urban forestry programs to demonstrate

Audience and objectives

their cost-effectiveness (McPherson 1995). If tree plantings are proven to benefit communities, then financial commitment to tree programs will be justified. Therefore, the objective of this tree guide is to identify and describe the benefits and costs of planting trees in Temperate Interior West communities—providing a tool for municipal tree managers, arborists, and tree enthusiasts to increase public awareness and support for trees (Dwyer and Miller 1999).

Chapter 2. Benefits and Costs of Urban and Community Forests

This chapter describes benefits and costs of public and privately managed trees and presents the functional benefits and associated economic value of community forests. Expenditures related to tree care and management are assessed—a necessary process for creating cost-effective programs (Dwyer et al. 1992, Hudson 1983).

Benefits

Saving Energy

Energy is an essential ingredient for quality of life and for economic growth. Conserving energy by greening our cities is often more cost-effective than building new power plants. For example, while California was experiencing energy shortages in 2001, its 177 million city trees were providing shade and conserving energy. Annual savings to utilities were an estimated $500 million in wholesale electricity and generation purchases (McPherson and Simpson 2003). Planting 50 million more shade trees in strategic locations would provide savings equivalent to seven 100-megawatt power plants. The cost of peak load reduction was $63 per kW, considerably less than the $150 per kW benchmark for cost-effectiveness. Utility companies in the Temperate Interior West and throughout the country can invest in shade tree programs as a cost-effective energy conservation measure to lower peak energy demands.

How trees work to save energy

Trees modify climate and conserve building energy use in three principal ways (fig. 3):

- Shading reduces the amount of heat absorbed and stored by built surfaces.

- Evapotranspiration converts liquid water to water vapor and thus cools the air by using solar energy that would otherwise result in heating of the air.

- Reducing windspeed reduces the infiltration of outside air into interior spaces and heat loss, especially where conductivity is relatively high (e.g., glass windows) (Simpson 1998).

Summer temperatures in cities can be 3 to 8 °F warmer than temperatures in the surrounding countryside. This is known as the **urban heat island** effect. Trees and other vegetation can combat this warming effect at small and large scales. On individual building sites, trees may lower air temperatures up to 5 °F compared with outside the **greenspace**. At larger scales (6 mi²), temperature differences of more than 9 °F have been observed between city centers and more vegetated suburban areas (Akbari et al. 1992). A recent study by scientists at National Aeronautics

Trees lower temperatures

Figure 3—Trees save energy for heating and cooling by shading buildings, lowering summertime temperatures, and reducing windspeeds. Secondary benefits from energy conservation are reduced water consumption and reduced pollutant emissions by power plants (drawing by Mike Thomas).

and Space Administration and Columbia University found that street trees provide the "greatest cooling potential per unit area" (Rosenzweig et al. 2006).

Trees increase home energy efficiency and save money

For individual buildings, strategically placed trees can increase energy efficiency in the summer and winter. Because the summer Sun is low in the east and west for several hours each day, solar angles should be considered (fig. 4). Trees that shade east and, especially, west walls help keep buildings cool. In the winter, allowing sunlight to strike the southern side of a building can warm interior spaces. However, the trunks and bare branches of **deciduous** trees that shade south- and east-facing walls during winter may increase heating costs by blocking 40 percent or more of winter sun (McPherson 1984).

Windbreaks reduce heat loss

Rates at which outside air infiltrates a building can increase substantially with windspeed. In cold, windy weather, the entire volume of air, even in newer or tightly sealed homes, may change every 2 to 3 hours. Windbreaks reduce windspeed and resulting air infiltration by up to 50 percent, translating into potential annual heating savings of 10 to 12 percent (Heisler 1986). Reductions in windspeed reduce heat transfer through conductive materials as well. Cool winter winds, blowing against windows, can contribute significantly to the heating load of buildings by increasing the gradient between inside and outside temperatures. Windbreaks reduce air infiltration and conductive heat loss from buildings. If located correctly,

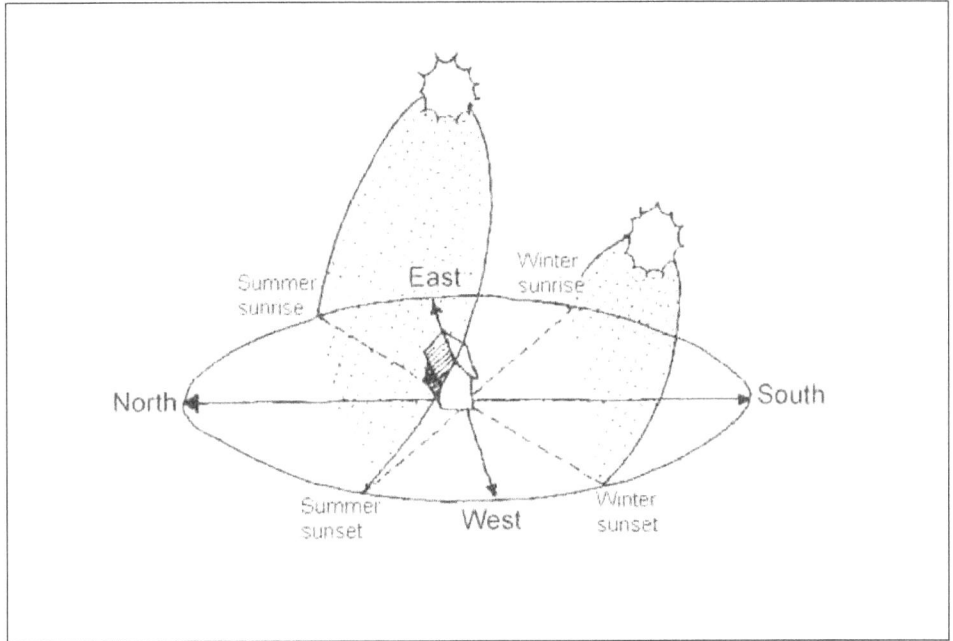

Figure 4—Paths of the sun on winter and summer solstices (from Sand 1991). Summer heat gain is primarily through east- and west-facing windows and walls. The roof receives most irradiance, but insulated attics reduce heat gain to living spaces. The winter sun, at a lower angle, strikes the south-facing surfaces.

trees planted as windbreaks can also serve as living snowfences, storing and directing the movement of snow (for more information see Brandle and Nickerson 1996).

Trees provide greater energy savings in the Temperate Interior West than in milder climate regions because they can have greater effects during the hot summers and cold winters. In Denver, for example, trees were found to produce substantial cooling savings for an energy-efficient two-story wood-frame house (McPherson et al. 1993). A typical energy-efficient house with air conditioning requires about $103 each year for cooling. A computer simulation demonstrated that three 25-ft tall trees—two on the west side of the house and one on the east—would save $35 each year for cooling, a 34-percent reduction (438 kWh).

A recent study of the municipal trees of Boise states that the 23,000 trees save city residents approximately $180,000 in annual air conditioning costs and $143,000 in heating costs (Peper et al., in press) or $13.88 per tree. The largest trees provide the largest benefits; the large silver maple (see "Common and Scientific Names" section), for example, accounts for 21 percent of the energy benefits although it represents only 8 percent of the population. In Reno, Nevada, early morning sunshine from the east can increase temperatures inside a home by as much as 20 °F in only a few hours. Carefully planted trees can help mitigate this effect and keep temperatures lower throughout the day (Post 2007).

Retrofit for more savings

Conserving energy by greening our cities is important because it can be more cost-effective than building new power plants (for more information, see the Center for Urban Forest Research's research summaries "Green Plants or Power Plants?" and "Save Dollars with Shade" [Geiger 2001, 2002a]). In the Temperate Interior West region, there is ample opportunity to "retrofit" communities with more sustainable landscapes through strategic tree planting and care of existing trees.

Reducing Atmospheric Carbon Dioxide

Trees reduce CO$_2$

Global temperatures have increased since the late 19th century, with major warming periods from 1910 to 1945 and from 1976 to the present (IPCC 2001). Human activities, primarily fossil-fuel consumption, are adding greenhouse gases to the atmosphere, and current research suggests that the recent increases in temperature can be attributed in large part to increases in greenhouse gases (IPCC 2001). Higher global temperatures are expected to have a number of adverse effects, including increasing the number and extent of wildfires, an aspect of particular concern in parts of the Temperate Interior West (McKenzie et al. 2004). Increasing frequency of extreme weather events will continue to tax emergency management resources.

Urban forests have been recognized as important storage sites for carbon dioxide (CO$_2$), the primary greenhouse gas (Nowak and Crane 2002). Private markets dedicated to reducing CO$_2$ emissions by trading carbon credits are emerging (Chicago Climate Exchange 2007, CO$_2$e.com 2007, McHale 2003). Carbon credits have sold for as much as EUR 33 per ton (about \$40; European Climate Exchange 2006), and the social costs of CO$_2$ emissions (an estimate of the monetary value of worldwide damage done by anthropogenic CO$_2$ emissions) are estimated to range from £4 to £27 per ton (\$7 to \$47 per ton) (Pearce 2003). For comparison, for every \$20 spent on a tree planting project in Arizona, 1 ton of atmospheric CO$_2$ was reduced (McPherson and Simpson 1999). As carbon trading markets become accredited and prices rise, these markets could provide monetary resources for community forestry programs.

Urban forests can reduce atmospheric CO$_2$ in two ways (fig. 5):

- Trees directly sequester CO$_2$ in their stems and leaves while they grow.

- Trees near buildings can reduce the demand for heating and air conditioning, thereby reducing emissions associated with power production.

Some tree-related activities release CO$_2$

At the same time, the positive impact of trees on CO$_2$ is offset by some emissions. To provide a complete picture of atmospheric CO$_2$ reductions from tree plantings, it is important to consider CO$_2$ released into the atmosphere through tree planting and care activities, as well as decomposition of wood from pruned or dead trees. During the process of planting and maintaining trees, vehicles, chain saws,

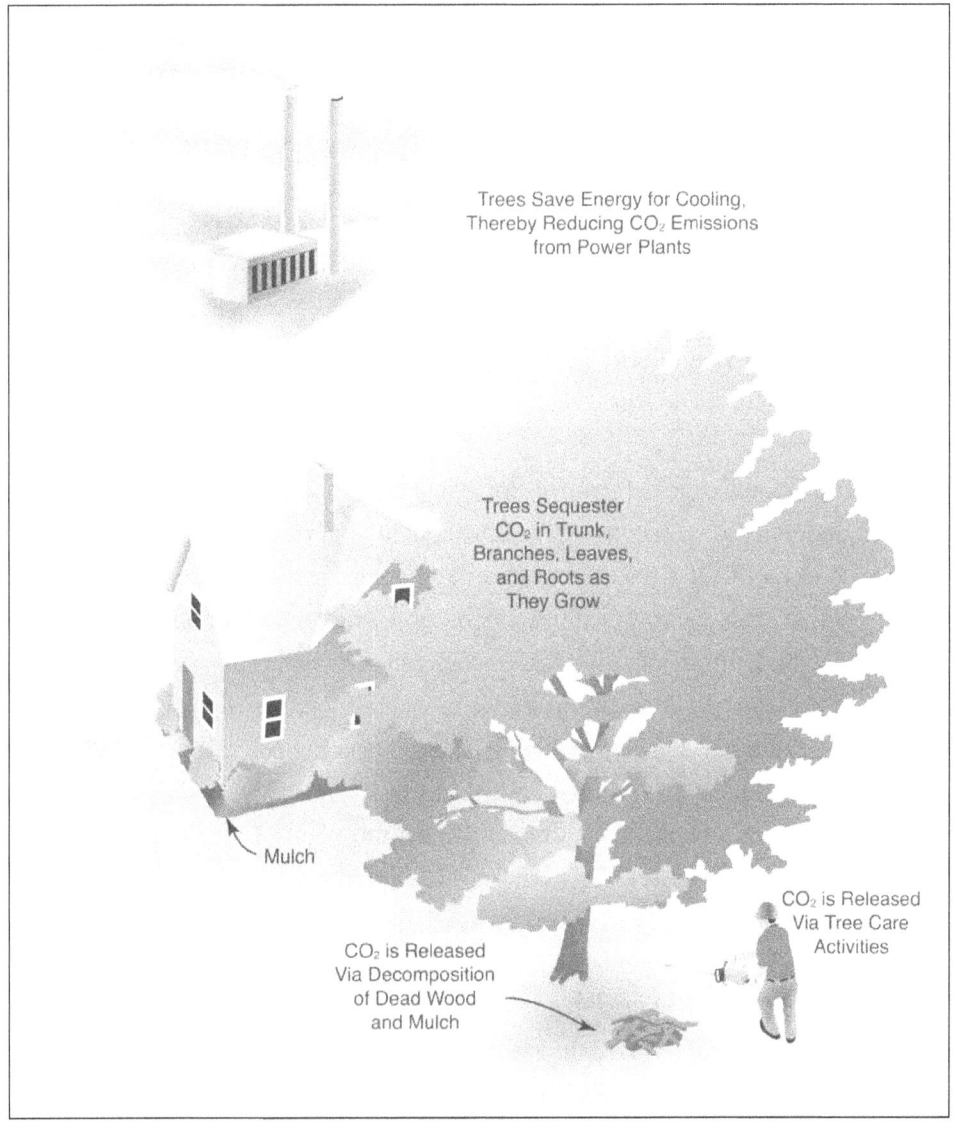

Trees Save Energy for Cooling,
Thereby Reducing CO_2 Emissions
from Power Plants

Trees Sequester
CO_2 in Trunk,
Branches, Leaves,
and Roots as
They Grow

Mulch

CO_2 is Released
Via Tree Care
Activities

CO_2 is Released
Via Decomposition
of Dead Wood
and Mulch

Figure 5—Trees sequester CO_2 as they grow and indirectly reduce CO_2 emissions from power plants through energy conservation. At the same time, CO_2 is released through decomposition and tree care activities that involve fossil-fuel consumption (drawing by Mike Thomas).

chippers, and other equipment release CO_2 (fig. 5). Typically, CO_2 released from tree planting, maintenance, and other tree-related activities is about 2 to 8 percent of annual CO_2 reductions obtained through sequestration and **reduced power plant emissions** (McPherson and Simpson 1999). And eventually, all trees die, and most of the carbon that has accumulated in their structure is released into the atmosphere as CO_2 through decomposition. The rate of release into the atmosphere depends on if and how the wood is reused. For instance, recycling of urban wood waste into products such as furniture can delay the rate of decomposition compared to its reuse as mulch. Tree waste can also be used as a fuel source to generate electricity.

If this biomass fuel replaces a more carbon-intensive form of electricity production, there will be an overall reduction in atmospheric CO_2.

Reduced CO_2 emissions

Regional variations in climate and the mix of fuels that produce energy to heat and cool buildings influence potential CO_2 emission reductions. The average emission rate in Boise, Idaho, is less than 1 lb of CO_2 per MWh (US EPA 2003), a very small amount, because 99.9 percent of Boise's power is generated hydroelectrically. Reno, Nevada, on the other hand, has an average emission of 1,861 lbs of CO_2 per MWh (US EPA 2003) because its power comes mainly from coal and natural gas. Cities in the Temperate Interior West with relatively high CO_2 emission rates will see greater benefits from reduced energy demand relative to other areas with lower emissions rates.

A study of the municipal trees of Boise found that the 23,000 publicly owned trees sequester about 1,121 tons of CO_2 (Peper et al., in press) annually. Approximately 215 tons of CO_2 is released from decaying trees and during maintenance, with a positive net reduction in atmospheric CO_2 owing to trees of 906 tons.

Another study in Chicago focused on the carbon sequestration benefit of residential tree canopy. Tree **canopy cover** in two residential neighborhoods was estimated to sequester on average 0.112 lb/ft^2, and pruning activities released 0.016 lb/ft^2 (Jo and McPherson 1995). Net annual carbon uptake was 0.096 lb/ft^2.

CO_2 reduction through community forestry

Grass-roots tree-planting efforts to reduce atmospheric CO_2 can be very successful. Since 1990, Trees Forever, an Iowa-based nonprofit organization, has planted trees for energy savings and atmospheric CO_2 reduction with utility sponsorships. Over 1 million trees have been planted in 400 communities with the help of 120,000 volunteers. These trees are estimated to offset CO_2 emissions by 50,000 tons annually. Based on an Iowa State University study, survival rates are an amazing 91 percent indicating a highly trained and committed volunteer force (Ramsay 2002).

Improving Air Quality

Trees improve air quality

Approximately 159 million people live in areas where ozone (O_3) concentrations violate federal air quality standards. About 100 million people live in areas where dust and other small particulate matter (PM_{10}) exceed levels for healthy air. Reno, Nevada, is among the cities listed in the U.S. EPA's (Environmental Protection Agency) Green Book (US EPA 2006) as being in violation of federal air quality standards for particulate matter. Air pollution is a serious health threat to many city dwellers, causing asthma, coughing, headaches, respiratory and heart disease, and cancer (Smith 1990). Impaired health results in increased social costs for medical care, greater absenteeism, and reduced longevity.

Recently, the EPA recognized tree planting as a measure in state implementation plans for reducing O_3. Air quality management districts have funded tree planting projects to control particulate matter. These policy decisions are creating new opportunities to plant and care for trees as a method for controlling air pollution (Luley and Bond 2002; for more information see www.treescleanair.org [USDA FS 2006b] and the Center for Urban Forest Research's research summary "Trees—The Air Pollution Solution" [Geiger 2006]).

Urban forests provide a number of air quality benefits:

- They absorb gaseous pollutants (e.g., O_3, nitrogen dioxide [NO_2], and sulfur dioxide [SO_2]) through leaf surfaces (fig. 6).

- They intercept PM_{10} (e.g., dust, ash, pollen, smoke) (fig. 6).

- They release oxygen through photosynthesis.

- They transpire water and shade surfaces, which lowers air temperatures, thereby reducing O_3 levels.

- They reduce energy use, which reduces emissions of pollutants from power plants, including NO_2, SO_2, PM_{10}, and volatile organic compounds (**VOCs**) (fig. 6).

- They shade paved surfaces and parked cars, reducing hydrocarbon emissions (fig. 6).

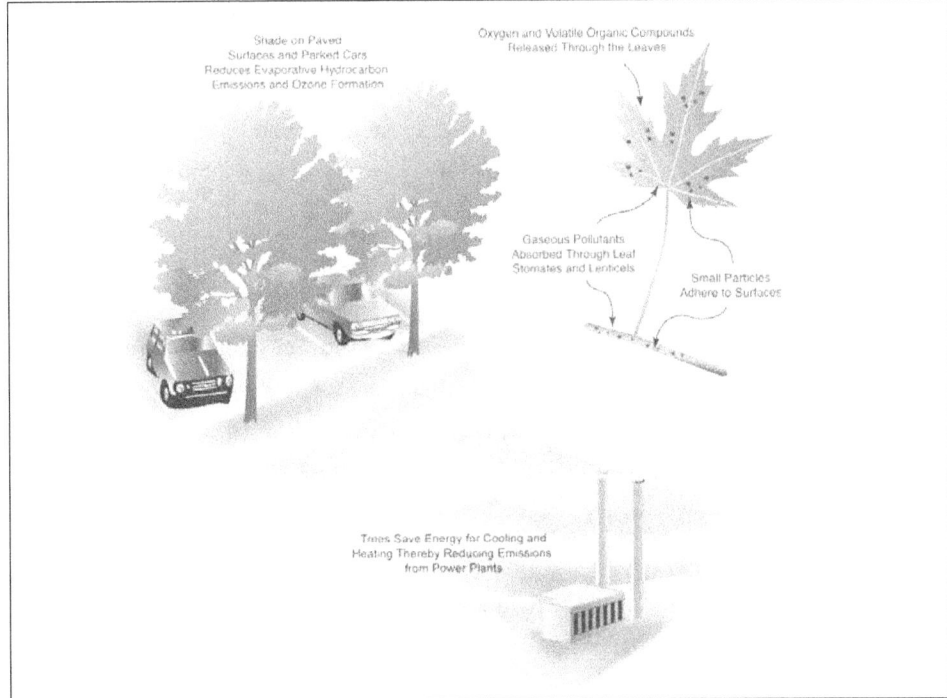

Figure 6—Trees absorb gaseous pollutants, retain particles on their surfaces, and release oxygen and volatile organic compounds. By cooling urban heat islands and shading parked cars, trees can reduce ozone formation (drawing by Mike Thomas).

**Trees influence
ozone formation**

Trees may also adversely affect air quality. Most trees emit **biogenic volatile organic compounds** (BVOCs) such as isoprenes and monoterpenes that can contribute to O_3 formation. The contribution of BVOC emissions from city trees to O_3 formation depends on complex geographic and atmospheric interactions that have not been studied in most cities. Some complicating factors include variations with temperature and atmospheric levels of NO_2.

A computer simulation study for Atlanta suggested that it would be very difficult to meet EPA ozone standards in the region by using trees because of the high BVOC emissions from native pines and other vegetation (Chameides et al. 1988). The results, however, were not straightforward. A later study showed that although removing trees reduced BVOC emissions, any positive effect was overwhelmed by increased hydrocarbon emissions from natural and anthropogenic sources owing to the increased air temperatures associated with tree removal (Cardelino and Chameides 1990). A similar finding was reported for the Houston-Galveston area, where deforestation associated with urbanization from 1992 to 2000 increased surface temperatures. Despite the decrease in BVOC emissions, O_3 concentrations increased because of the enhanced urban heat island effect during simulated episodes (Kim et al. 2005).

As well, the O_3-forming potential of tree species differs considerably (Benjamin and Winer 1998). Trees emitting the greatest relative amount of BVOCs are sweetgum, blackgum, sycamore, poplar, and oak (Nowak 2000). In a study in the Los Angeles basin, increased planting of low-BVOC-emitting tree species was shown to reduce O_3 concentrations, whereas planting of medium and high emitters would increase overall O_3 concentrations (Taha 1996). A study in the Northeastern United States, however, found that species mix had no detectable effects on O_3 concentrations (Nowak et al. 2000). Although new trees increased BVOC emissions, ambient VOC emissions were so high that additional BVOCs had little effect on air quality. These potentially negative effects of trees on one kind of air pollution must be considered in light of their great benefit in other areas.

**Trees absorb
gaseous pollutants**

Trees absorb gaseous pollutants through stomates, tiny openings in the leaves. Other methods of pollutant removal include adsorption of gases to plant surfaces and uptake through bark pores. Once gases enter the leaf they diffuse into intercellular spaces, where some react with inner leaf surfaces and others are absorbed by water films to form acids. Pollutants can damage plants by altering their metabolism and growth. At high concentrations, pollutants cause visible damage to leaves, such as spotting and bleaching (Costello and Jones 2003). Although some pollutants may pose health hazards to plants, pollutants such as nitrogenous gases can also be sources of essential nutrients for them.

Trees intercept small airborne particles. Some particles that are intercepted by a tree are absorbed, but most adhere to plant surfaces. Species with hairy or rough leaf, twig, and bark surfaces are efficient interceptors (Smith and Dochinger 1976). Intercepted particles are often resuspended to the atmosphere when wind blows the branches, and rain will wash some particulates off plant surfaces. The ultimate fate of these pollutants depends on whether they fall onto paved surfaces and enter the stormwater system, or fall on pervious surfaces, where they are filtered in the soil.

Trees intercept particulate matter

Trees near buildings can reduce the demand for heating and air conditioning, thereby reducing emissions of PM_{10}, SO_2, NO_2, and VOCs associated with electric power production, an effect that can be sizable. For example, a strategically located tree can save 100 kWh in electricity for cooling annually (McPherson and Simpson 1999, 2002, 2003). Assuming that this conserved electricity comes from a typical new coal-fired power plant in the Temperate Interior West, the tree reduces emissions of SO_2 by 1.25 lb, NO_2 by 0.39 lb (US EPA 2003), and PM_{10} by 0.84 lb (US EPA 1998). The same tree is responsible for conserving 60 gal of water in cooling towers and reducing CO_2 emissions by 200 lb.

In the nearby Willamette/Lower Columbia River Valley of Washington and Oregon, the tree **canopy** over nearly 8 million acres was estimated to remove 178 million lbs of air pollutants annually with a value of $419 million (American Forests 2001). A substantial decline in overall canopy cover from 46 percent in 1972 to 24 percent in 2001 owing to increased development has meant a corresponding decline in air quality benefits, which were estimated retrospectively (in today's dollars) at $719 million for 1972. Chicago's 50.8 million trees were estimated to remove 234 tons of PM_{10}, 210 tons of O_3, 93 tons of SO_2, and 17 tons of carbon monoxide in 1991. This environmental service was valued at $9.2 million (Nowak 1994).

Trees in a Davis, California, parking lot were found to improve air quality by reducing air temperatures 1 to 3 °F (Scott et al. 1999). By shading asphalt surfaces and parked vehicles, trees reduce hydrocarbon emissions (VOCs) from gasoline that evaporates out of leaky fuel tanks and worn hoses (for more information, see our research summary "Where Are All the Cool Parking Lots?" [Geiger 2002b]). These evaporative emissions are a principal component of smog, and parked vehicles are a primary source (fig. 7). In California, parking-lot tree plantings can be funded as an air quality improvement measure because of the associated reductions in evaporative emissions.

Shade from trees prevents evporative hydrocarbon emission

Reducing Stormwater Runoff and Improving Hydrology

Urban stormwater runoff is a major source of pollution entering wetlands, streams, lakes, and oceans. Healthy trees can reduce the amount of runoff and pollutants

Figure 7—Trees planted to shade parking areas can reduce hydrocarbon emissions and improve air quality.

in receiving waters (Cappiella et al. 2005). This is important because federal law requires states and localities to control nonpoint-source pollution, such as runoff from pavements, buildings, and landscapes. Trees are mini-reservoirs, controlling runoff at the source, thereby reducing runoff volumes and erosion of watercourses, as well as delaying the onset of **peak flows**. Trees can reduce runoff in several ways (fig. 8; for more information, see our research summary "Is All Your Rain Going Down the Drain?" [Geiger 2003]):

- Leaves and branch surfaces intercept and store rainfall, thereby reducing runoff volumes and delaying the onset of peak flows.

- Roots reduce soil compaction, increasing the rate at which rainfall infiltrates soil and the capacity of soil to store water, reducing overland flow.

- Tree canopies reduce soil erosion by diminishing the impact of raindrops on barren surfaces.

- **Transpiration** through tree leaves reduces moisture levels in the soil, increasing the soil's capacity to store rainfall.

Trees reduce runoff

Rainfall that is stored temporarily on canopy leaf and bark surfaces is called intercepted rainfall. Intercepted water evaporates, drips from leaf surfaces, and flows down stem surfaces to the ground. Tree surface saturation generally occurs after 1 to 2 in of rain has fallen (Xiao et al. 2000). During large storm events, rain-

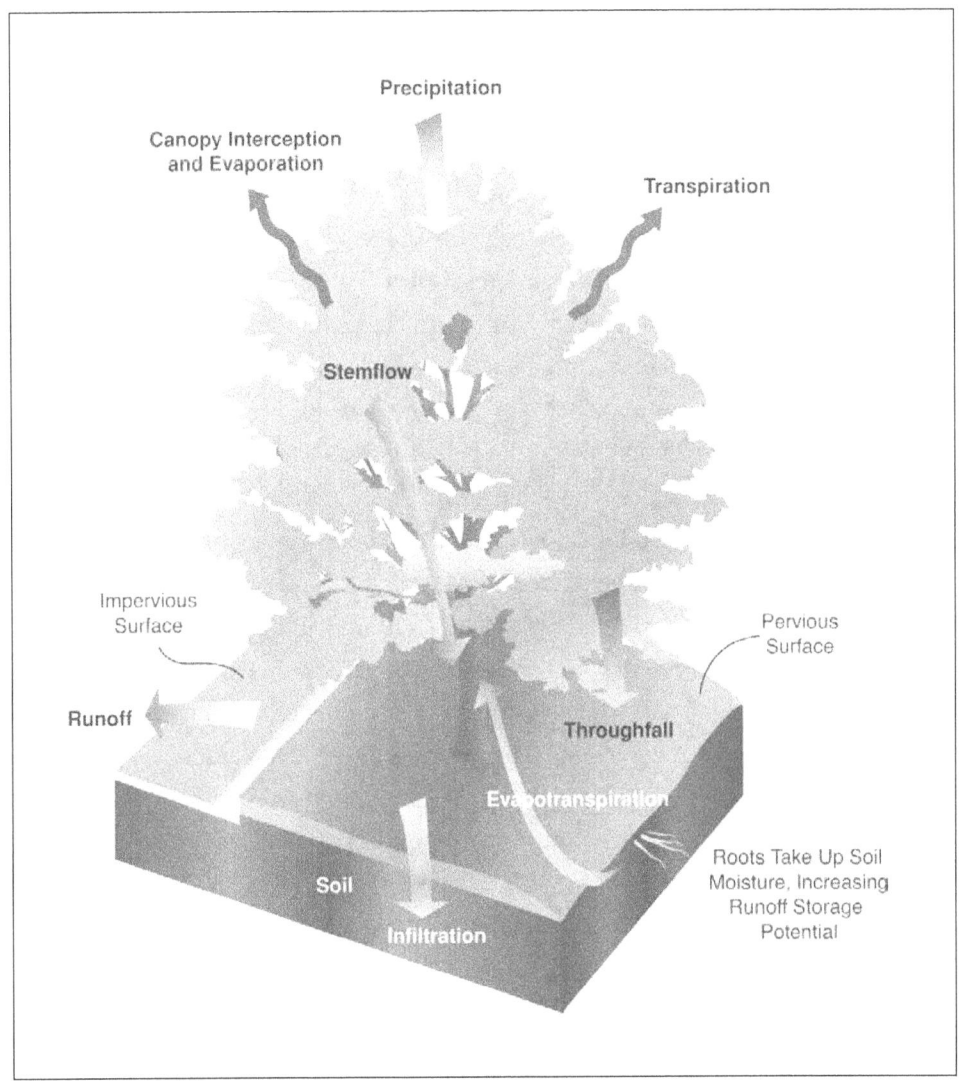

Figure 8—Trees intercept a portion of rainfall that evaporates and never reaches the ground. Some rainfall runs to the ground along branches and stems (stemflow) and some falls through gaps or drips off leaves and branches (throughfall). Transpiration increases soil moisture storage potential (drawing by Mike Thomas).

fall exceeds the amount that the tree crown can store, about 50 to 100 gal per tree. The interception benefit is the amount of rainfall that does not reach the ground because it evaporates from the crown. As a result, the volume of runoff is reduced and the time of peak flow is delayed. Trees protect water quality by substantially reducing runoff during small rainfall events that are responsible for most pollutant washoff. Therefore, urban forests generally produce more benefits through water quality protection than through flood control (Xiao et al. 1998, 2000).

The amount of rainfall trees intercept depends on their architecture, rainfall patterns, and climate. Tree-crown characteristics that influence interception are the trunk, stem, and surface areas, textures, area of gaps, period when leaves are present, and dimensions (e.g., tree height and diameter). Trees with coarse surfaces retain more rainfall than those with smooth surfaces. Large trees generally intercept more rainfall than small trees do because greater surface areas allow for greater evaporation rates. Tree crowns with few gaps reduce **throughfall** to the ground. Species that are in leaf when rainfall is plentiful are more effective than deciduous species that have dropped their leaves during the rainy season.

Studies that have simulated urban forest effects on stormwater runoff have reported reductions of 2 to 7 percent. Annual interception of rainfall by Sacramento's urban forest for the total urbanized area was only about 2 percent because of the winter rainfall pattern and sparsity of **evergreen** species (Xiao et al. 1998). However, average interception in canopied areas ranged from 6 to 13 percent (150 gal per tree), similar to values reported for rural forests. Broadleaf evergreens and **conifers** intercept more rainfall than deciduous species in areas where rainfall is highest in fall, winter, or spring (Xiao and McPherson 2002).

In Albuquerque, a city with approximately half the rainfall of the Temperate Interior West region, the canopy of the 21,000 municipal park trees reduced runoff by more than 11 million gal, with an estimated value of $56,000 (Vargas et al. 2006). In contrast, in Montgomery, Alabama, a city with about half as many people but many more trees and approximately 50 in more rain than Albuquerque, the tree canopy was estimated to reduce runoff by 1.7 billion gal, valued at $454 million per 20-year construction cycle (American Forests 2004). According to a recent study, the 23,000 municipal trees of Boise, Idaho, were estimated to intercept approximately 19.2 million gal of stormwater annually, with an estimated value of $96,000 (Peper et al., in press).

Urban forests can treat wastewater

Urban forests can provide other hydrologic benefits, too. For example, tree plantations, nurseries, or landscapes can be irrigated with partially treated wastewater. Infiltration of water through the soil can be a safe and productive means of water treatment. Reused wastewater applied to urban forest lands can recharge aquifers, reduce stormwater-treatment loads, and create income through sales of nursery or wood products. Recycling urban wastewater into greenspace areas can be an economical means of treatment and disposal while at the same time providing other environmental benefits (USDA NRCS 2005).

Aesthetics and Other Benefits

Beautification

Trees provide a host of aesthetic, social, economic, and health benefits that should be included in any benefit-cost analysis. One of the most frequently cited reasons that people plant trees is for beautification. Trees add color, texture, line, and form to the landscape, softening the hard geometry that dominates built environments. Research on the aesthetic quality of residential streets has shown that street trees are the single strongest positive influence on scenic quality (Schroeder and Cannon 1983).

In surveys, consumers have shown greater preference for commercial streetscapes with trees. In contrast to areas without trees, shoppers shop more often and longer in well-landscaped business districts. They are willing to pay more for parking and up to 11 percent more for goods and services (Wolf 1999).

Attractiveness of retail settings

Research in public housing complexes found that outdoor spaces with trees were used significantly more often than spaces without trees. By facilitating interactions among residents, trees can contribute to reduced levels of domestic violence, as well as foster safer and more sociable neighborhood environments (Sullivan and Kuo 1996).

Public safety benefits

Well-maintained trees increase the "curb appeal" of properties (fig. 9). Research documenting the increase in dollar value that can be attributed to trees is difficult to conduct and is still in early stages, but some studies comparing sales prices of residential properties having different numbers of trees have suggested that people are willing to pay 3 to 7 percent more for properties with ample trees versus few or no trees. One of the most comprehensive studies of the influence of trees on home property values was based on actual sales prices and found that each large front-yard tree was associated with about a 1-percent increase in sales price (Anderson and Cordell 1988). A much greater value of 9 percent ($15,000) was determined

Property value benefits

Figure 9—Trees beautify a neighborhood, increasing property values and creating a more sociable environment.

in a U.S. Tax Court case for the loss of a large black oak on a property valued at $164,500 (Neely 1988). Depending on average home sales prices, the value of this benefit can contribute significantly to cities' property tax revenues.

Social and psychological benefits

Scientific studies confirm that trees in cities provide social and psychological benefits. Humans derive substantial pleasure from trees, whether it is inspiration from their beauty, a spiritual connection, or a sense of meaning (Dwyer et al. 1992, Lewis 1996). After natural disasters, people often report a sense of loss if their community forest has been damaged (Hull 1992). Views of trees and nature from homes and offices provide restorative experiences that ease mental fatigue and help people to concentrate (Kaplan and Kaplan 1989). Desk workers with a view of nature report lower rates of sickness and greater satisfaction with their jobs compared to those having no visual connection to nature (Kaplan 1992). Trees provide important settings for recreation and relaxation in and near cities. The act of planting trees can have social value, as bonds between people and local groups often result.

Human health benefits

A series of studies on human stress caused by general urban conditions show that views of nature reduce the stress response of both body and mind (Parsons et al. 1998), improving general well-being. Urban green also appears to have a positive effect on the human immune system. Hospitalized patients who have views of nature and spend time outdoors need less medication, sleep better, have a better outlook, and recover more quickly than patients without connections to nature (Ulrich 1985). Skin cancer is a particular concern in the sunny Temperate Interior West region. By providing shade, trees reduce exposure to ultraviolet (UV) light, thereby lowering the risk of harmful effects from skin cancer and cataracts (Tretheway and Manthe 1999). At the latitudes of the Temperate Interior West, the ultraviolet protection factor provided by trees increases from approximately 2 under a 30-percent canopy cover to approximately 15 under a 90-percent canopy cover (Grant et al. 2002). Because early exposure to UV radiation is a risk factor for later development of skin cancer, planting trees around playgrounds, schools, day care centers, and ball fields can be especially valuable in helping reduce the risk of later-life cancers.

Noise reduction

Certain environmental benefits from trees are more difficult to quantify than those previously described, but can be just as important. Noise can reach unhealthy levels in cities. Trucks, trains, and planes can produce noise that exceeds 100 decibels (dB), twice the level at which noise becomes a health risk. Thick strips of vegetation in conjunction with landforms or solid barriers can reduce some highway noise and have a psychological effect (Cook 1978), but if vegetation is used as the only sound barrier, the amount necessary to achieve measurable reductions in noise (about 200 ft for a 10-dB reduction) may be impractical (U.S. Department of Transportation 1995). Other studies have shown that the performance of noise barriers is increased when used in combination with vegetative screens (van Rentergehm et al. 2002).

Numerous types of wildlife inhabit cities and are generally highly valued by residents. For example, older parks, cemeteries, and botanical gardens often contain a rich assemblage of wildlife. Remnant woodlands and riparian habitats within cities can connect a city to its surrounding bioregion (fig. 10). Wetlands, greenways (linear parks), and other greenspace can provide habitats that conserve biodiversity (Platt et al. 1994).

Wildlife habitat

Urban forestry can provide jobs for both skilled and unskilled labor. Public service programs and grassroots-led urban and community forestry programs provide horticultural training to volunteers across the United States. Also, urban and community forestry provides educational opportunities for residents who want to learn about nature through firsthand experience (McPherson and Mathis 1999). Local nonprofit tree groups and municipal volunteer programs often provide educational material and hands-on training in the care of trees and work with area schools.

Jobs and environmental education

Tree shade on streets can help offset the cost of managing pavement by protecting it from weathering. The asphalt paving on streets contains stone aggregate in an oil binder. Tree shade lowers the street surface temperature and reduces heating and volatilization of the binder (McPherson and Muchnick 2005). As a result, the aggregate remains protected for a longer period by the oil binder.

Shade can reduce street maintenance

Figure 10—Natural areas within cities are refuges for wildlife and help connect city dwellers with their ecosystems.

Figure 11—Although shade trees can be expensive to maintain, their shade can reduce the costs of resurfacing streets (McPherson and Muchnick 2005), promote pedestrian travel, and improve air quality directly through pollutant uptake and indirectly through reduced emissions of volatile organic compounds from cars.

When unprotected, vehicles loosen the aggregate, and much like sandpaper, the loose aggregate grinds down the pavement. Because most weathering of asphalt-concrete pavement occurs during the first 5 to 10 years when new street tree plantings provide little shade, this benefit mainly applies when older streets are resurfaced (fig. 11). In snowier communities, the benefit from summer shade can be offset by winter shade that prolongs snow and ice accumulation, and may result in greater use of salt and sand. Further study is needed to evaluate the seasonal effects of tree shade on paving condition and safety.

Costs

Muncipal costs of tree care

The environmental, social, and economic benefits of urban and community forests come, of course, at a price. A national survey reported that communities in the Temperate Interior West region spent an average of about $6.39 per tree, in 1994, for street- and park-tree management (Tschantz and Sacamano 1994). This amount is relatively high, with only three national regions spending more than this and six regions spending less. Nationwide, the single largest expenditure was for tree pruning, followed by tree removal/disposal, and tree planting. The survey did not include non-tree-care costs, such as money spent on infrastructure repair, litigation, and cleanup.

Our survey of **municipal foresters** in Boise, Lewiston, Nampa, Payette, and Caldwell, Idaho, and Carson City, Nevada, indicates that they are spending about $18 per tree annually. The greatest costs are for pruning ($5 to $7 per tree) and planting ($4 per tree). Removal and disposal ($2 to $3 per tree) and administration ($3 per tree) are the next most costly.

Annual expenditures for tree management on private property have not been well documented. Costs differ considerably, ranging from some commercial or residential properties that receive regular professional landscape service to others that are virtually "wild" and without maintenance. Our survey of commercial arborists in the Temperate Interior West indicated that expenditures typically range from $8 to $11 per tree. Expenditures are usually greatest for pruning, planting, and removal.

Residental costs differ

Planting and Maintaining Trees

Planting costs include the cost of the tree and the cost for planting, staking, and mulching. Based on our survey of Temperate Interior West municipal and commercial arborists, planting costs differ with tree size and range from $75 for a 1.5-in diameter at breast height (d.b.h.) tree to $250 for a 2-in d.b.h. tree. Pruning cycles differ by city and by tree size and range from once every 2 to 4 years for new trees to once in 5 to 10 years for large, mature trees. The cost for pruning young trees ranged from $25 to $50 for a public tree and from $35 to $45 for a yard tree; the cost to prune a large, mature tree was about $250 for public trees and ranged from $80 to $400 for yard trees.

Because of the region's hot and dry summer climate, most trees require irrigation throughout their lives, but because most are planted into areas that are already irrigated, such as parkways or other landscaped areas, the cost for additional water for the trees is negligible and is ignored for the purposes of this guide. Newly planted trees, however, require additional watering in early years to successfully establish themselves. The costs of irrigation for public trees are estimated at about $1.50 for the first 5 years, mainly for the labor costs involved in visiting the trees with a water truck or other time-intensive methods. No additional costs are included for establishment watering of yard trees, as the few minutes of labor necessary is considered negligible.

At the end of a tree's life, removal costs can be substantial, especially for large trees. Removal and disposal of small trees (under 3 in d.b.h.) cost between $10 and $50, but a large tree may cost several thousand dollars to remove. According to our survey, total costs for removal of trees and stumps are approximately $34 per in d.b.h. for yard trees and $27 per in d.b.h. for public trees.

Conflicts With Urban Infrastructure

Tree roots can damage sidewalks

Like other cities across the United States, communities in the Temperate Interior West region are spending millions of dollars each year to manage conflicts between trees and power lines, sidewalks, sewers, and other elements of the urban infrastructure. According to our survey, cities in the region are spending about $1 to $4 per tree annually on sidewalk, curb, and gutter repair costs. This amount is far less than the $11.22 per tree reported for 18 California cities (McPherson 2000). In addition, the figures for California apply only to street trees and do not include repair costs for damaged sewer lines, building foundations, parking lots, and various other **hardscape** elements.

In some cities, decreasing budgets are increasing the sidewalk-repair backlog and forcing cities to shift the costs of sidewalk repair to residents. This shift has significant impacts on residents in older areas, where large trees have outgrown small sites and infrastructure has deteriorated. It should be noted that trees are not always fully responsible for these problems. In older areas, in particular, sidewalks and curbs may have reached the end of their 20- to 25-year service life, or may have been poorly constructed in the first place (Sydnor et al. 2000).

Costs of conflicts

Efforts to control the costs of these conflicts are having alarming effects on urban forests (Bernhardt and Swiecki 1993, Thompson and Ahern 2000):

- Cities are downsizing their urban forests by planting smaller trees. Although small trees are appropriate under power lines and in small planting sites, they are less effective than large trees at providing shade, absorbing air pollutants, and intercepting rainfall.

- Thousands of healthy urban trees are lost each year and their benefits forgone because of sidewalk damage, the second most common reason that street and park trees were removed.

- Most cities surveyed were removing more trees than they were planting. Residents forced to pay for sidewalk repairs may not want replacement trees.

Cost-effective strategies to retain benefits from large street trees while reducing costs associated with infrastructure conflicts are described in Reducing Infrastructure Damage by Tree Roots (Costello and Jones 2003). Matching the growth characteristics of trees to the conditions at the planting site is one important strategy.

Tree roots can also damage old sewer lines that are cracked or otherwise susceptible to invasion. Sewer repair companies estimate that sewer damage is minor until trees and sewers are over 30 years old, and roots from trees in yards are usually more of a problem than roots from trees in planter strips along streets. The latter assertion may be because the sewers are closer to the root zone as they enter houses than at the street. Repair costs typically range from $100 for sewer rodding (inserting a cleaning implement to temporarily remove roots) to $1,000 or more for sewer excavation and replacement.

Most communities sweep their streets regularly to reduce surface-runoff pollution entering local waterways. Street trees drop leaves, flowers, fruit, and branches year round that constitute a significant portion of debris collected from city streets. When leaves fall and rains begin, **tree litter** can clog sewers, dry wells, and other elements of flood-control systems. Costs include additional labor needed to remove leaves, and property damage caused by localized flooding. Wind and ice storms also incur cleanup costs.

The cost of addressing conflicts between trees and power lines is reflected in electric rates. Large trees under power lines require more frequent pruning than better suited trees, which can make large trees appear less attractive (fig. 12). Frequent crown reduction reduces the benefits these trees could otherwise provide. Moreover, increased costs for pruning are passed on to customers.

Cleaning up after trees

Large trees under power lines can be costly

Figure 12—Large trees planted under power lines can require extensive pruning, which increases tree care costs and reduces the benefits of those trees, including their appearance.

The green infrastructure is a significant component of communities in the Interior West region. The urban tree canopy of Boise, Idaho is shown here.

Chapter 3. Benefits and Costs of Community Forests in Temperate Interior West Communities

This chapter presents estimated benefits and costs for trees planted in typical residential yards and public sites. Because benefits and costs differ with tree size, we report results for representative small, medium, and large deciduous trees and for a representative conifer.

Estimates are initial approximations, as some benefits and costs are intangible or difficult to quantify (e.g., impacts on psychological health, crime, and violence). Limited knowledge about physical processes at work and their interactions makes estimates imprecise (e.g., fate of air pollutants trapped by trees and then washed to the ground by rainfall). Tree growth and mortality rates are highly variable throughout the region. Benefits and costs also differ, depending on differences in climate, pollutant concentrations, maintenance practices, and other factors. Given the Temperate Interior West region's diverse landscape, with different climates, soils, and types of community forestry programs, the approach used here provides first-order approximations. It is a general accounting that can be easily adapted and adjusted for local planting projects. It provides a basis for decisions that set priorities and influence management direction (Maco and McPherson 2003).

Overview of Procedures

Approach

In this study, annual benefits and costs are estimated over a 40-year planning horizon for newly planted trees in three residential yard locations (east, south, and west of the residence) and a public streetside or park location (app. 2). Henceforth, we refer to trees in these hypothetical locations as "yard" trees and "public" trees, respectively. Prices are assigned to each cost (e.g., planting, pruning, removal, irrigation, infrastructure repair, liability) and benefit (e.g., heating/cooling energy savings, air pollutant mitigation, stormwater runoff reduction, and aesthetic and other benefits measured as increases in property value) through direct estimation and implied valuation of benefits as environmental externalities. This approach makes it possible to estimate the net benefits of plantings in "typical" locations by using "typical" tree species. More information on data collection, modeling procedures, and assumptions can be found in appendix 3.

To account for differences in the mature size and growth of different tree species, we report results for a small (crabapple), medium (Norway maple), and large (white ash) deciduous tree and a conifer (blue spruce) (figs. 13 to 16) (see "Common and Scientific Names" section). The conifer is assumed to be a windbreak tree located more than 50 ft from the residence so it does not shade the building. The

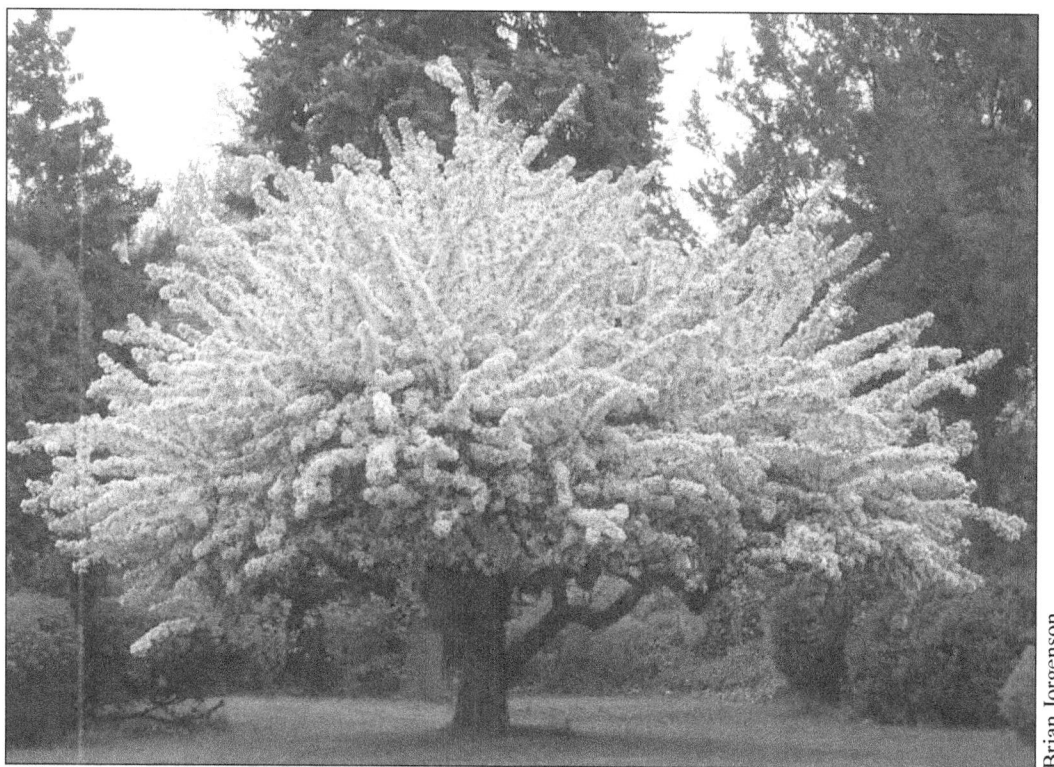

Figure 13—The crabapple represents small trees in this guide.

Figure 14—The Norway maple represents medium trees in this guide.

Figure 15—The white ash represents large trees in this guide.

Figure 16—The blue spruce represents coniferous trees in this guide.

selection of these species is based on data availability and representative growth and is not intended to endorse their use in large numbers. In fact, white ash is susceptible to the emerald ash borer, which may become a serious threat to all ash trees in the region.

Tree dimensions are derived from growth curves developed from park and street trees in Boise, Idaho (Peper et al., in press) (fig. 17).

Frequency and costs of tree management are estimated based on surveys with municipal foresters from Boise, Lewiston, Nampa, Payette, and Caldwell, Idaho, and Carson City, Nevada. In addition, several commercial arborists from Boise and Meridian, Idaho, provided information on tree management costs on residential properties.

Tree care costs based on survey findings

Benefits are calculated with numerical models and data both from the region (e.g., pollutant emission factors for avoided emissions from energy savings) and from local sources (e.g., Boise climate data for energy effects). Regional electricity and natural gas prices are used in this study to quantify energy savings. **Damage costs** and **control costs** are used to estimate **willingness to pay**. For example, the

Tree benefits based on numerical models

27

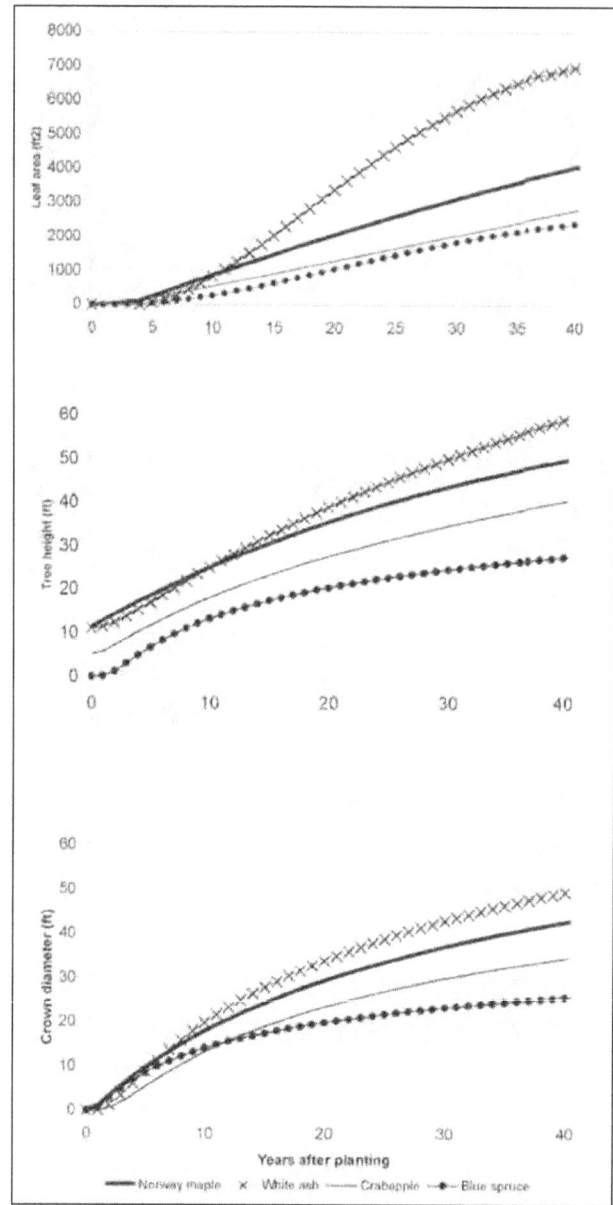

Figure 17—Tree growth curves are based on data collected from park trees in Boise, Idaho. Data for representative small, medium, large, and conifer trees are for the crabapple, Norway maple, white ash, and blue spruce, respectively. Differences in leaf surface area among species are most important for this analysis because functional benefits such as summer shade, rainfall interception, and pollutant uptake are related to leaf area.

value of stormwater runoff reduction owing to rainfall interception by trees is estimated by using marginal control costs. If a community or developer is willing to pay an average of $0.01 per gal of treated and controlled runoff to meet minimum standards, then the stormwater runoff mitigation value of a tree that intercepts 1,000 gal of rainfall, eliminating the need for control, should be $10.

Reporting Results

Results are reported in terms of annual value per tree planted. To make these calculations realistic, however, mortality rates are included. Based on our survey of regional municipal foresters and commercial arborists, this analysis assumes that 43 percent of the planted trees will die over the 40-year period. Annual mortality rates are 2.6 percent per year for the first 5 years and 0.85 percent per year for the remainder of the 40-year period. This accounting approach "grows" trees in different locations and uses computer simulation to calculate the annual flow of benefits and costs as trees mature and die (McPherson 1992). In appendix 2, results are reported at 5-year intervals for 40 years.

Tree mortality included

Findings of This Study

Average Annual Net Benefits

Average annual net benefits (benefits minus costs) per tree over a 40-year period increase with mature tree size (for detailed results see app. 2):

Average annual net benefits increase wtih tree size

- $12 to $24 for a small tree

- $29 to $45 for a medium tree

- $47 to $63 for a large tree

- $22 to $25 for a conifer

Our findings demonstrate that average annual net benefits from large trees like the white ash are substantially greater than those from small trees like the crabapple. Average annual net benefits for the small, medium, and large deciduous public trees are $12, $30, and $49, respectively. Conifers provide an intermediate level of benefits, on average $22 for a public tree. The largest average annual net benefits, however, stem from yard trees opposite the west-facing wall of a house: $24, $45, $63, and $25, for small, medium, and large deciduous trees and the conifer, respectively.

Large trees provide the most benefits

At year 40, the large yard tree opposite a west wall produces a net annual benefit of $69. In the same location, 40 years after planting, the crabapple, Norway maple, and blue spruce produce annual net benefits of $35, $57, and $34. Forty years after planting at a typical public site, the small, medium, and large deciduous trees and the conifer provide annual net benefits of $18, $39, $50, and $28, respectively.

Net benefits for a yard tree opposite a west house wall and a public tree also increase with size when summed over the entire 40-year period:

Net benefits summed over 40 years

- $953 (yard) and $479 (public) for a small tree

- $1,784 (yard) and $1,184 (public) for a medium tree

- $2,497 (yard) and $1,931 (public) for a large tree
- $984 (yard) and $840 (public) for a conifer

Year 20 environmental benefits exceed tree care costs

Even just 20 years after planting, average annual benefits for all trees exceed costs of tree planting and management (tables 1 and 2). For a large white ash in a yard 20 years after planting, the total value of environmental benefits alone ($51) is more than 10 times the total annual cost ($5). Environmental benefits total $24, $41, and $23 for the crabapple, Norway maple, and blue spruce, and tree care costs are comparable across species, $5, $5, and $3, respectively. Adding the value of aesthetics and other benefits to the environmental benefits results in even greater net benefits.

Net benefits for public trees at 20 years ($20, $36, $69, and $26 for small, medium, and large deciduous trees and the conifer; table 2) are less than yard trees ($32, $53, $85, and $31) for two main reasons: public tree care costs are greater because public trees generally receive more intensive care than private trees; and energy benefits are lower for public trees than for yard trees because public trees are assumed to provide general climate effects, but not to shade buildings directly.

Average Annual Costs

Costs of tree care

Averaged over 40 years, the costs for yard and public trees, respectively, are as follows:

- $8 and $16 for a small tree
- $10 and $18 for a medium tree
- $11 and $19 for a large tree
- $7 and $12 for a conifer

Annualized over the 40-year period, tree planting is the single greatest cost for yard trees, averaging $4 per tree per year (see app. 2). Based on our survey, we assume in this study that a 2-in diameter at breast height (d.b.h.) yard tree is planted at a cost of $175. The cost for planting a 2-in d.b.h. public tree is $140. For public trees, where safety is particularly important and conflicts with infrastructure are greater, pruning is the greatest cost, with average annual costs of $1 to $7. Annual pruning costs for yard trees are also significant at $1 to $4. Removal and disposal costs, annualized over 40 years, average $2 to $3 per tree. At $2 to $3 per tree per year, administrative costs are significant for public trees.

Table 3 shows annual management costs 20 years after planting for yard trees to the west of a house and for public trees. Annual costs for yard trees range from $3 to $5, and public tree care costs are $9 to $14. In general, public trees are more expensive to maintain than yard trees because of their prominence and because of the greater need for public safety.

Table 1—Estimated annual benefits and costs for a private tree (residential yard) opposite the west-facing wall 20 years after planting

Benefit category	Crabapple small tree 20 ft tall 23-ft spread LSA = 1,039 ft²		Norway maple medium tree 35 ft tall 29-ft spread LSA = 2,114 ft²		White ash large tree 39 ft tall 34-ft spread LSA = 3,376 ft²		Blue spruce conifer tree 28 ft tall 20-ft spread LSA = 1,331 ft²	
	Resource units	Total value	Resource units	Total value	Resource units	Total value	Resource units	Total value
		Dollars		*Dollars*		*Dollars*		*Dollars*
Electricity savings ($0.0820/kWh)	179 kWh	14.68	329 kWh	26.97	395 kWh	32.42	71.4 kWh	5.85
Natural gas savings ($1.17/therm)	6.26 therms	7.30	6.99 therms	8.16	9.17 therms	10.69	7.69 therms	8.97
Carbon dioxide ($0.00334/lb)	260 lb	0.87	412 lb	1.38	466 lb	1.55	161.3 lb	0.54
Ozone ($0.51/lb)	0.18 lb	0.09	0.28 lb	0.14	0.62 lb	0.32	0.21 lb	0.11
Nitrogen dioxide ($0.51/lb)	0.33 lb	0.17	0.53 lb	0.27	0.71 lb	0.36	0.24 lb	0.12
Sulfur dioxide ($0.06 /lb)	0.65 lb	0.04	1.16 lb	0.07	1.45 lb	0.09	0.37 lb	0.02
Small particulate matter ($0.92/lb)	0.18 lb	0.17	0.25 lb	0.23	0.48 lb	0.44	0.16 lb	0.15
Volatile organic compounds ($0.14/lb)	0.06 lb	0.01	0.10 lb	0.01	0.13 lb	0.02	0.04 lb	0
Biogenic volatile organic compounds ($0.14/lb)	0 lb	0	-0.14 lb	-0.02	0 lb	0	-1.34 lb	-0.19
Rainfall interception ($0.005/gal)	142 gal	0.71	796 gal	3.98	993 gal	4.96	1,390 gal	6.95
Environmental subtotal		24.04		41.19		50.86		22.54
Other benefits		12.60		16.68		39.37		11.12
Total benefits		36.63		57.87		90.24		33.66
Total costs		4.58		5.12		5.20		2.91
Net benefits		32.05		52.74		85.04		30.74

LSA = leaf surface area.

Table 2—Estimated annual benefits and costs for a public tree (street/park) 20 years after planting

Benefit category	Crabapple small tree 20 ft tall 23-ft spread LSA = 1,039 ft²		Norway maple medium tree 35 ft tall 29-ft spread LSA = 2,114 ft²		White ash large tree 39 ft tall 34-ft spread LSA = 3,376 ft²		Blue spruce conifer tree 28 ft tall 20-ft spread LSA = 1,331 ft²	
	Resource units	Total value	Resource units	Total value	Resource units	Total value	Resource units	Total value
		Dollars		*Dollars*		*Dollars*		*Dollars*
Electricity savings ($0.0820/kWh)	99 kWh	5.19	329 kWh	26.97	395 kWh	32.42	71.4 kWh	5.85
Natural gas savings ($1.17/therm)	7.47 therms	8.72	10.46 therms	12.20	12.67 therms	14.78	7.69 therms	8.97
Carbon dioxide ($0.00334/lb)	215 lb	0.63	412 lb	1.38	466 lb	1.55	161.3 lb	0.54
Ozone ($0.51/lb)	0.18 lb	0.15	0.28 lb	0.14	0.62 lb	0.32	0.21 lb	0.11
Nitrogen dioxide ($0.51/lb)	0.33 lb	0.30	0.53 lb	0.27	0.71 lb	0.36	0.24 lb	0.12
Sulfur dioxide ($0.06 /lb)	0.65 lb	0.57	1.16 lb	0.07	1.45 lb	0.09	0.37 lb	0.02
Small particulate matter ($0.92/lb)	0.18 lb	0.29	0.25 lb	0.23	0.48 lb	0.44	0.16 lb	0.15
Volatile organic compounds ($0.14/lb)	0.06 lb	0.02	0.10 lb	0.01	0.13 lb	0.02	0.04 lb	0
Biogenic volatile organic compounds ($0.14/lb)	0 lb	- 0.27	-0.14 lb	-0.02	0 lb	0	-1.34 lb	-0.19
Rainfall interception ($0.005/gal)	142 gal	1.30	796 gal	3.98	993 gal	4.96	1,390 gal	6.95
Environmental subtotal		10.74		41.19		50.86		22.54
Other benefits		2.75		16.68		39.37		11.12
Total benefits		13.49		57.87		90.24		33.66
Total costs		12.50		14.14		14.37		8.68
Net benefits		20.35		35.52		68.94		26.27

LSA = leaf surface area.

Average Annual Benefits

Average annual benefits, including stormwater reduction, aesthetic value, air quality improvement and carbon dioxide (CO_2) sequestration increase with mature tree size (figs. 18 and 19; for detailed results see app. 2):

- $25 to $32 for a small tree

- $39 to $55 for a medium tree

- $58 to $74 for a large tree

- $32 to $33 for a conifer

Energy benefits are greatest

Energy Savings—

Energy benefits are greatest and tend to increase with mature tree size. For example, average annual net energy benefits over the 40-year period are $21 for the small crabapple tree opposite a west-facing wall, and $39 for the larger white ash. For species of all sizes, energy savings increase as trees mature and their leaf surface area increases (figs. 18 and 19).

Table 3—Estimated annual costs 20 years after planting for a private tree opposite the west-facing wall and a public tree

Costs	Crabapple small tree 20 ft tall 23-ft spread LSA = 1,039 ft²		Norway maple medium tree 35 ft tall 29-ft spread LSA = 2,114 ft²		White ash large tree 39 ft tall 34-ft spread LSA = 3,376 ft²		Blue spruce conifer tree 28 ft tall 20-ft spread LSA = 1,331 ft²	
	Private: west	Public tree	Private: west	Public tree	Private: west	Public tree	Private: west	Public tree
	Dollars per tree per year							
Pruning	2.30	5.56	2.30	5.56	2.30	5.56	0.23	0.56
Remove and dispose	1.87	2.23	2.31	2.75	2.37	2.83	2.19	2.61
Pest and disease	0.15	0.13	0.18	0.15	0.19	0.16	0.17	0.15
Infrastructure	0.21	1.40	0.25	1.73	0.26	1.77	0.24	1.64
Cleanup	0.06	0.41	0.07	0.50	0.08	0.52	0.07	0.48
Liability and legal	0.01	0.04	0.01	0.05	0.01	0.06	0.01	0.05
Admin. and other	0	2.74	0	3.39	0	3.48	0	3.21
Total costs	4.58	12.50	5.12	14.14	5.20	14.37	2.91	8.68
Total benefits	36.63	32.85	57.87	49.66	90.24	83.30	33.66	34.96
Total net benefits	32.05	20.35	52.74	35.52	85.04	68.94	30.74	26.27

Note: Prices for removal and disposal are included to account for expected mortality of citywide planting.

LSA = leaf surface area.

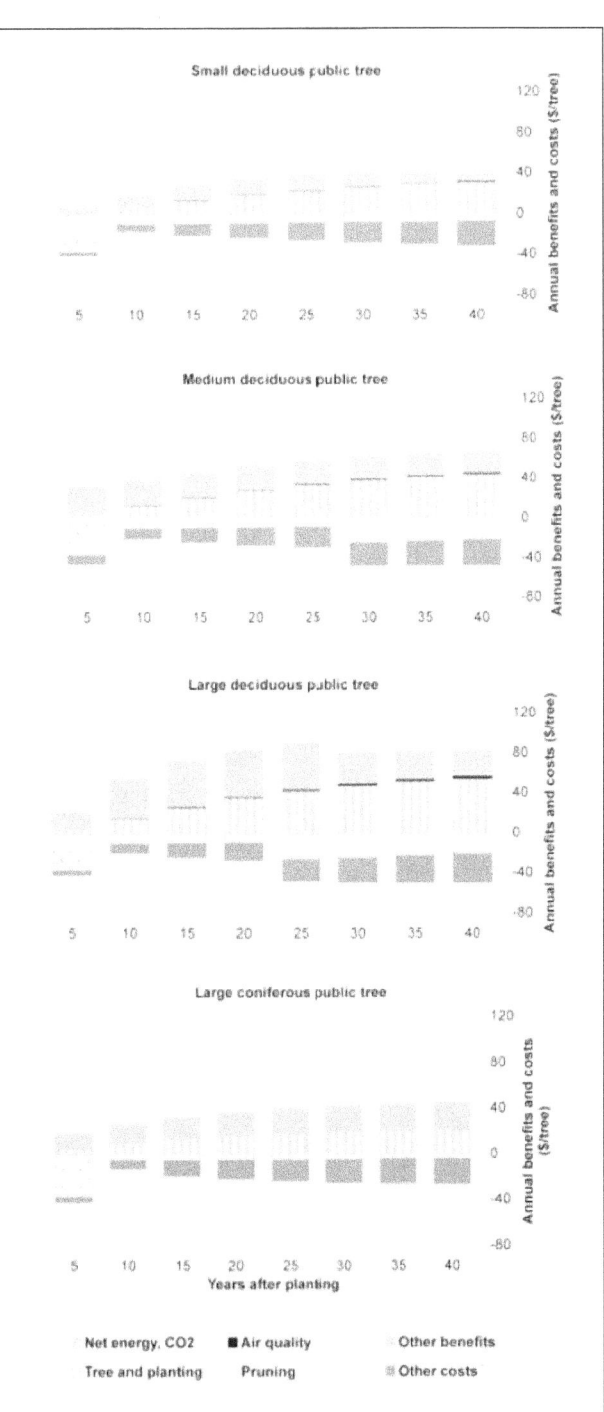

Figure 18— Estimated annual benefits and costs for a small (apple), medium (Norway maple), and large (white ash) deciduous tree, and a conifer (blue spruce) located west of a residence. Costs are greatest during the initial establishment period whereas benefits increase with tree size.

Figure 19— Estimated annual benefits and costs for public small (apple), medium (Norway maple), and large (white ash) deciduous tree, and a conifer (blue spruce).

As might be expected in a region with hot, dry summers and cold winters, both cooling and heating savings are substantial. Trees planted on the west side of buildings have the greatest total energy benefits because the effect of shade on cooling costs is maximized without blocking the warming rays of the winter sun. A yard tree located south of a home produced the least total energy benefit because it had the least benefit during the summer and the greatest adverse effect from shade on heating costs in winter. Trees located east of a building provided intermediate benefits. Total energy benefits also reflect species-related traits such as size, form, branch pattern, and density, as well as time in leaf.

Average annual total energy benefits for public trees were less than for yard trees and ranged from $14 for the blue spruce to $30 for the large white ash.

Aesthetic and Other Benefits—

Aesthetic and other benefits reflected in property values account for a significant portion of total benefits. As trees grow and become more visible, they can increase a property's sales price. Annual values averaged over 40 years associated with these aesthetic and other benefits for yard trees are $9, $16, $26, and $10 for the small, medium, and large deciduous trees and for the conifer, respectively. The values for public trees are $10, $18, $29, and $12, respectively. The values for yard trees are slightly less than for public trees because off-street trees contribute less to a property's curb appeal than more prominent street trees. Because our estimates are based on median home sale prices, the effects of trees on property values and aesthetics will differ depending on local economies.

Stormwater Runoff Reduction—

By intercepting rain and snow before it reaches the stormwater treatment system, trees can have a valuable effect on reducing runoff. The white ash intercepts 1,111 gal per year on average over a 40-year period with an implied value of $6. The crabapple, Norway maple, and blue spruce intercept 161, 893, and 1,459 gal per year on average, with values of $1, $4, and $7, respectively. Forty years after planting, average stormwater runoff reductions equal 309, 1,663, 2,102, and 2,463 for the small, medium, and large deciduous trees and the conifer, respectively.

As the cities of the Temperate Interior West continue to grow, the amount of impervious surface will continue to increase dramatically. The role that trees, in combination with other strategies such as rain gardens and structural soils, can play in reducing stormwater runoff is substantial.

Air Quality Improvement—

Air quality benefits are defined as the sum of pollutant uptake by trees and avoided power plant emissions from energy savings minus biogenic volatile organic

Aesthetic benefits are substantial

compounds (BVOCs) released by trees. Average annual air quality benefits over the 40-year period were approximately $1 per tree. These relatively low air quality benefits reflect the clean air of most cities in the Temperate Interior West region. The benefits in terms of avoided emissions, for instance, are quite low, because much of the energy in the region is produced from clean sources such as hydroelectric plants. Contrast these results with the air quality benefits of a large tree in the Northeast region ($13; McPherson et al., in press), Midwest region ($7.65; McPherson et al. 2006c), and southern California ($28.38; McPherson 2000).

The ability of trees to intercept particulate matter (PM_{10}) from the air is the most highly valued. Over 40 years, the white ash, for example, is estimated to reduce an average of 0.59 lb of PM_{10} from the air annually, valued at $0.54. Average annual reductions in nitrogen dioxide, ozone, sulfur dioxide, and volatile organic compounds for the large tree are valued at $0.35, $0.36, $0.08, and $0.02, respectively.

Forty years after planting, the average annual monetary values of air quality improvement for the crabapple tree, Norway maple, white ash, and blue spruce are $0.80, $1.21, $2.50, and $0.11, respectively.

Carbon Dioxide Reduction—

Net atmospheric CO_2 reductions accrue for all tree types. Average annual net reductions range from a high of 436 lbs ($1.46) for a large tree on the west side of a house to a low of 194 lbs ($0.65) for a small tree on the southern side of the house. Deciduous trees opposite west-facing house walls generally produce the greatest CO_2 reduction because of reduced power plant emissions associated with energy savings. The values for the crabapple tree are lowest for CO_2 reduction reflecting this small tree's minor effect on energy savings and sequestration.

Forty years after planting, net CO_2 benefits for a yard tree opposite a west wall are 420, 543, 638, and 195 lbs for the small, medium, and large deciduous trees and the conifer, respectively. Releases of CO_2 associated with tree care activities account for less than 1 percent of net CO_2 sequestration.

Brian Jorgenson

In the Temperate Interior West region, trees play an environmental, cultural, and historical role in communities.

Chapter 4. Estimating Benefits and Costs for Tree Planting Projects in Your Community

This chapter shows two ways that benefit-cost information presented in this guide can be used. The first hypothetical example demonstrates how to adjust values from the guide for local conditions when the goal is to estimate benefits and costs for a proposed tree planting project. The second example explains how to compare net benefits derived from planting different types of trees. The last section discusses actions communities can take to increase the cost-effectiveness of their tree programs.

Applying Benefit-Cost Data

Chinook Valley Example

The hypothetical city of Chinook Valley is located in the Temperate Interior West region and has a population of 24,000. Most of its street trees were planted decades ago, with English elms and silver maples (see "Common and Scientific Names" section) as the dominant species. Currently, the tree canopy cover is sparse because a number of trees died after drought conditions made them more susceptible to pests, and they have not been replaced. Many of the remaining street trees are in declining health. The city hired an urban forester 2 years ago and an active citizens' group, the Green Team, has formed (fig. 20).

Figure 20—The (hypothetical) Green Team is motivated to re-green their community by planting 1,000 trees in 5 years.

Initial discussions among the Green Team, local utilities, the urban forester, and other partners led to a proposed urban forestry program. The program intends to plant 1,000 trees in Chinook Valley over a 5-year period. Trained volunteers will plant 3-in diameter trees in the following proportions: 70 percent large-maturing trees, 15 percent medium-maturing trees, 5 percent small-maturing trees, and 10 percent conifers. One hundred trees will be planted in parks, and the remaining 900 trees will be planted along Main Street and other downtown streets. Mortality rates for earlier planting projects have been high, so the Green Team and the urban forester will concentrate their planting efforts in areas that are likely to be most successful, including planting spaces with sufficient soil capacity for trees to grow and as little conflict with infrastructure as possible, and that maximize environmental benefits. They expect to find a number of good suggestions for planting in chapter 5 of this guide.

The Chinook Valley City Council has agreed to maintain the current funding level for management of existing trees. Also, they will advocate formation of a municipal tree district to raise funds for the proposed tree-planting project. A municipal tree district is similar in concept to a landscape assessment district, which receives revenues based on formulas that account for the services different customers receive. For example, the proximity of customers to greenspace in a landscape assessment district may determine how much they pay for upkeep. A municipal tree district might receive funding from air quality districts, stormwater management agencies, electric utilities, businesses, and residents in proportion to the value of future benefits these groups will receive from trees in terms of air quality, hydrology, energy, carbon dioxide (CO_2), and property value. The formation of such a district would require voter approval of a special assessment that charges recipients for tree planting and maintenance costs in proportion to the benefits they receive from the new trees. The council needs to know the amount of funding required for tree planting and maintenance, as well as how the benefits will be distributed over the 40-year life of the project.

The first step: determine tree planting numbers

As a first step, the Chinook Valley city forester and Green Team decided to use the tables in appendix 2 to quantify total cumulative benefits and costs over 40 years for the proposed planting of 1,000 public trees—700 large, 150 medium, and 50 small deciduous trees and 100 conifers.

Before setting up a spreadsheet to calculate benefits and costs, the team considered which aspects of Chinook Valley's urban and community forestry project differ from the regional values used in this guide (the methods for calculating the values in app. 2 are described in app. 3):

1. The prices of electricity and natural gas in Chinook Valley are $0.06 per kWh and $1.05 per therm, not $0.082 per kWh and $1.17 per therm as used in this guide. It is assumed that the buildings that will be shaded by the new street trees have air conditioning and natural-gas heating.

2. The Green Team projected future annual costs for monitoring tree health and implementing their stewardship program. Administration costs are estimated to average $2,500 annually for the life of the trees or $2.50 per tree each year. This guide assumed an average annual administration cost of about $3.00 per tree. Thus, an adjustment is necessary.

3. Planting will cost $200 per tree. The guide assumes planting costs of $140 per tree. The costs will be slightly higher for Chinook Valley because they have decided to plant larger trees.

To calculate the dollar value of total benefits and costs for the 40-year period, the forester created a spreadsheet table (table 4). Each benefit and cost category is listed in the first column. Prices, adjusted where necessary for Chinook Valley, are entered into the second column. The third column contains the **resource units** (RUs) per tree per year associated with the benefit or the cost per tree per year, which can be found in appendix 2. For aesthetic and other benefits, the dollar values for public trees are placed in the RU columns. The fourth column lists the 40-year total values, obtained by multiplying the RU values by tree numbers, prices, and 40 years.

The second step: adjust for local prices of benefits

To adjust for higher electricity prices, the forester multiplied electricity saved for a large public tree in the RU column (209 kWh) by the Chinook Valley price for electricity ($0.06/kWh). This value ($12.54 per tree per year) was multiplied by the number of trees planted and 40 years ($12.54 × 700 trees × 40 years = $351,120) to obtain cumulative air-conditioning energy savings for the large public trees (table 4). The process was carried out for all benefits and all tree types.

To adjust cost figures, the city forester changed the planting cost from $140 assumed in the guide to $200 (table 4). This planting cost was annualized by dividing the cost per tree by 40 years ($200/40 = $5.00 per tree per year). Total planting costs were calculated by multiplying this value by 700 large trees and 40 years ($140,000).

The third step: adjust for local costs

The administration, inspection, and outreach costs are expected to average $2.50 per tree per year. Consequently, the total administration cost for large trees is $2.50 × 700 large trees × 40 years ($70,000). The same procedure was followed to calculate costs for the medium and small trees and conifers.

Table 4—Spreadsheet calculations of benefits and costs for the Chinook Valley planting project (1,000 trees) over 40 years

Benefits	Adjusted price	50 small trees		150 medium trees		700 large trees		100 conifer trees		1,000 total trees		
		Resource units	Total value	Resource units	Total value	Resource units	Total value	Resource units	Total value	Resource units	Total value	Percentage of benefits
	Dollars	*Resource units per tree per year*	*Dollars*	*Resource units per tree per year*	*Dollars*	*Resource units per tree per year*	*Dollars*	*Resource units per tree per year*	*Dollars*	*Resource units per tree per year*	*Dollars*	*Percent*
Electricity (kWh)	0.0600	100	12,000	160	57,600	209	351,120	67	16,080	10.92	436,800	20.2
Natural gas (therms)	1.05	6.91	14,511	9.62	60,606	11.17	328,398	7.05	29,610	10.83	433,125	20.0
Net carbon dioxide (lb)	0.00334	214	1,430	313	6,273	358	33,480	150	2,004	1.08	43,187	2.0
Ozone (lb)	0.51	0.20	204	0.31	949	0.70	9,996	0.22	449	0.29	11,598	2.0
Nitrogen dioxide (lb)	0.51	0.33	337	0.52	1,591	0.69	9,853	0.23	469	0.31	12,250	
Sulfur dioxide (lb)	0.06	0.66	79	1.13	407	1.39	2,335	0.34	82	0.07	2,903	
Small particulate matter (lb)	0.92	0.17	313	0.27	1,490	0.59	15,198	0.17	626	0.44	17,627	
Volatile organic compounds (lb)	0.14	0.06	17	0.10	84	0.12	470	0.03	17	0.01	588	
Biogenic volatile organic compounds (lb)	0.14	0	0	-0.16	-134	0	0	-1.94	-1,086	-0.03	-1,220	
Hydrology (gal)	0.0050	161	1,610	893	26,790	1,111	155,540	1,459	29,180	5.33	213,120	9.9
Aesthetics and other		9.76	19,520	17.87	107,220	29.32	820,960	11.54	46,160	24.85	993,860	45.9
Total benefits			50,003		262,800		1,726,949		123,567	54.09	2,163,319	100.0

Costs		Per tree	Total value	Per tree	Total value	Per tree	Total value	Per tree	Total value	Per tree	Total value	Percentage of costs
		Dollars per tree per year	*Dollars*	*Dollars per tree per year*	*Dollars*	*Dollars per tree per year*	*Dollars*	*Dollars per tree per year*	*Dollars*	*Dollars per tree per year*	*Dollars*	*Percent*
Tree and planting		5.00	10,000	5.00	30,000	5.00	140,000	5.00	20,000	5.00	200,000	27.0
Pruning		5.42	10,840	6.52	39,120	6.97	195,160	0.50	2,019	6.18	247,162	33.5
Remove and dispose		2.22	4,440	2.72	16,320	2.77	77,560	2.51	10,040	2.71	108,360	14.7
Infrastructure repair		1.28	2,562	1.57	9,400	1.60	44,773	1.45	5,786	1.56	62,520	8.5
Irrigation		0.37	740	0.46	2,760	0.47	13,160	0.42	1,680	0.46	18,340	2.5
Cleanup		0.04	80	0.05	300	0.05	1,400	0.05	200	0.05	1,980	0.3
Admin. and other		2.50	5,000	2.50	15,000	2.50	70,000	2.50	10,000	2.50	100,000	13.6
Total costs			33,673		112,905		542,080		49,707	18.46	738,269	100.0
Net benefit			16,343		149,880		1,184,869		73,847	35.64	1,424,939	
Benefit/cost ratio			1.49		2.33		3.19		2.49		2.93	

RU = resource unit.

All costs and all benefits were summed. Annual benefits over 40 years for the whole planting total $2.16 million ($54.10 per tree per year), and annual costs total about $740,000 ($18.46 per tree per year). Subtracting total costs from total benefits yields net benefits over the 40-year period:

- $16,343 or $8.17 per tree per year for small deciduous trees
- $149,880 or $24.98 per tree per year for medium deciduous trees
- $1,184,869 or $42.32 per tree per year for large deciduous trees
- $73,847 or $18.46 per tree per year for conifers

Dividing total benefits by total costs yielded benefit-cost ratios (BCRs) of 1.49 for small trees, and 2.33, 3.19, and 2.49 for medium and large deciduous trees and conifers. The BCR for the entire planting is 2.93, indicating that $2.93 will be returned for every $1 invested.

This analysis assumes 43 percent of the planted trees die and does not account for the time value of money from a capital investment perspective. Use the municipal discount rate to compare this investment in tree planting and management with alternative municipal investments.

The city forester and Green Team now know that the project will cost about $740,000, and the average annual cost will be $18,500 ($740,000/40 years); however, a higher proportion of funds will be needed initially for planting and irrigation. The fifth and last step is to identify the distribution of functional benefits that the trees will provide. The last column in table 4 shows the distribution of benefits as a percentage of the total:

- Energy savings = 40 percent (cooling = 20 percent, heating = 20 percent)
- CO_2 reduction = 2 percent
- Stormwater runoff reduction = 10 percent
- Air quality improvement = 2 percent
- Aesthetics/property value increase = 46 percent

With this information the planning team can determine how to distribute the costs for tree planting and maintenance based on who benefits from the services the trees will provide. For example, assuming the goal is to generate enough annual revenue to cover the total costs of managing the trees ($740,000), fees could be distributed in the following manner:

- $296,000 from electric and natural gas utilities for peak energy savings (40 percent). (Utility companies invest in planting trees because it is more cost effective to reduce peak energy demand than to meet peak needs through added infrastructure.)

The fourth step: calculate net benefits and benefit-cost ratio for public trees

The final step: determine how benefits are distributed and link these to sources of revenue

Distributing costs of tree management to multiple parties

- $15,000 from local industry for atmospheric CO_2 reductions (2 percent).

- $74,000 from the stormwater management district for water quality improvement associated with reduced runoff (10 percent).

- $15,000 from air quality management district for net reduction in air pollutants (2 percent).

- $340,000 from property owners for increased property values (46 percent).

Whether funds are sought from partners, the general fund, or other sources, this information can assist managers in developing policy, setting priorities, and making decisions. The Center for Urban Forest Research has developed a computer program called STRATUM that simplifies these calculations for analysis of existing street tree populations (Maco and McPherson 2003; for more information, see USDA FS 2006a).

City of Solanum Example

As a municipal cost-cutting measure, the hypothetical city of Solanum plans to stop planting street trees in areas of new development. Instead, developers will be required to plant front yard trees, thereby reducing costs to the city. The community forester and concerned citizens believe that, although this policy will result in lower planting costs, developers may plant smaller trees than the city would have. Currently, Solanum's policy is to plant as large a tree as possible based on each site's available growing space (fig. 21). Planting smaller trees could result in benefits "forgone" that will exceed cost savings. To evaluate this possible outcome, the community forester and concerned citizens decided to compare costs and benefits of planting small, medium, and large trees for a hypothetical street-tree planting project in Solanum.

The first step: calculate benefits and costs over 40 years

As a first step, the city forester and concerned citizens decided to quantify the total cumulative benefits and costs over 40 years for a typical street tree planting of 1,500 trees in Solanum. For comparison purposes, the planting includes 500 small trees, 500 medium trees, and 500 large trees. Data in appendix 2 are used for the calculations; however, three aspects of Solanum's urban and community forestry program are different from those assumed in this tree guide:

1. The price of electricity is $0.075/kWh, not $0.082/kWh.

2. The city will provide irrigation for the first 5 years at a cost of approximately $0.50 per tree annually.

3. Planting costs are $225 per tree for city trees instead of $140 per tree.

To calculate the dollar value of total benefits and costs for the 40-year period, the last column in the appendix 2 tables (40-year average) is multiplied by 40 years.

Figure 21— A policy such as Solanum's, to plant as large a tree as the site will handle, has provided ample benefits in the past. Here, large-growing trees are being planted.

Because this value is for one tree it must be multiplied by the total number of trees planted in the respective small, medium, or large tree size classes. To adjust for higher electricity prices, we multiply electricity saved per tree in the RU column (tables 6, 9, 12, and 15) for each tree type by the number of trees and 40 years (large tree: 209 kWh × 500 trees × 40 years = 4,180,000 kWh). This value is multiplied by the price of electricity in Solanum ($0.075/kWh × 4,180,000 kWh = $313,500) to obtain cumulative air-conditioning energy savings for the project (table 5).

All the benefits are summed for each size tree for a 40-year period. The 500 small trees provide $530,400 in total benefits. The medium and large trees provide approximately $924,200 and $1.3 million, respectively.

To adjust cost figures, we add a value for irrigation by multiplying the annual cost by the number of trees and by the number of years that irrigation will be applied ($0.50 × 500 trees × 5 years = $1,250). We multiply 500 large trees by the unit planting cost ($225) to obtain the adjusted cost for planting (500 × $225 = $100,000). The average annual 40-year costs taken from appendix 2 for other items are multiplied by 40 years and the appropriate number of trees to compute total

The second step: adjust for local prices of benefits

The third step: adjust for local costs

costs. These 40-year cost values are entered into table 5. The total costs for the small, medium and large trees are $338,050, $389,050, and $401,250.

Subtracting total costs from total benefits yields net benefits for the small ($192,350), medium ($535,150), and large ($895,500) trees. The total net benefits for the 40-year period are $1.6 million (total benefits - total costs), or $1,082 per tree on average (table 5).

The net benefits per public tree over the 40-year period are as follows:

- $385 for a small tree
- $1,070 for a medium tree
- $1,791 for a large tree

Table 5—Spreadsheet calculations of benefits and costs for the Solanum planting project (1,500 trees) over 40 years

Benefits	500 small		500 medium		500 large		1,500 tree total		Average value per tree
	RUs	Total value	RUs	Total value	RUs	Total value	RUs	Total value	
		Dollars		Dollars		Dollars		Dollars	Dollars
Electricity (kWh)	2,000,000	150,000	3,200,000	240,000	4,180,000	313,500	9,380,000	703,600	469
Natural gas (therms)	138,200	145,200	192,400	202,000	223,400	234,600	554,000	581,800	388
Net carbon dioxide (lb)	4,280,000	14,200	6,260,000	20,800	7,160,000	24,000	17,700,000	59,000	39
Ozone (lb)	4,030	2,000	6,270	3,200	13,930	7,200	24,230	12,400	8
Nitrogen dioxide (lb)	6,610	3,400	10,440	5,400	13,790	7,000	30,840	15,800	11
Sulfur dioxide (lb)	13,240	800	22,670	1,400	27,890	1,600	63,800	3,800	3
Small particulate matter (lb)	3,450	3,200	5,400	5,000	11,800	10,800	20,650	19,000	13
Volatile organic compounds (lb)	1,180	200	1,980	200	2,440	400	5,600	800	1
Biogenic volatile organic compunds (lb)	-70	0	-3,290	-400	0	0	-3,360	-400	0
Hydrology (gal)	3,220,000	16,200	17,860,000	89,200	22,220,000	111,200	43,300,000	216,600	144
Aesthetics and other benefits		195,200		357,400		586,400		1,139,000	759
Total benefits		530,400		924,200		1,296,700		2,751,400	1,834

Costs	Total value	Total value	Total value	Total value	Average value per tree
	Dollars	Dollars	Dollars	Dollars	Dollars
Tree and planting	100,000	100,000	100,000	300,000	200
Pruning	108,400	130,400	139,400	378,200	252
Remove and dispose	44,400	54,400	55,400	154,200	103
Infrastructure	25,600	31,400	32,000	89,000	59
Irrigation	1,250	1,250	1,250	3,750	3
Cleanup	7,400	9,200	9,400	26,000	17
Liability and legal	800	1,000	1,000	2,800	2
Admin. and other	50,200	61,400	62,800	174,400	116
Total costs	338,050	389,050	401,250	1,128,350	752
Net benefits	192,350	535,150	895,500	1,623,050	1,082
Benefit-cost ratio	1.57	2.38	3.23	2.44	

RU = resource unit.

By not investing in street tree planting, the city would save $300,000 in initial planting costs. If the developer planted 1,500 small trees, benefits would total $1.6 million (3 × $530,400 for 500 small trees). If 1,500 large trees were planted, benefits would total $3.9 million. Planting all small trees causes the city to forgo benefits valued at $2.3 million. This amount far exceeds the savings of $300,000 obtained by requiring developers to plant new street trees, and suggests that, when turning over the responsibility for tree planting to others, the city would benefit by developing and enforcing a street tree ordinance that requires planting large trees where feasible.

Based on this analysis, the City of Solanum decided to retain the policy of promoting planting of large trees where space permits and require tree shade plans that show how developers will achieve 50 percent shade over streets, sidewalks, and parking lots within 15 years of development.

The fourth step: calculate cost saving and benefits forgone

This analysis assumes that 43 percent of the planted trees died. It does not account for the time value of money from a capital investment perspective, but this could be done by using the municipal discount rate.

Increasing Program Cost-Effectiveness

What if the program you have designed looks promising in terms of stormwater-runoff reduction, energy savings, volunteer participation, and additional benefits, but the costs are too high? This section describes some steps to consider that may increase benefits and reduce costs, thereby increasing cost-effectiveness.

What if costs are too high?

Increasing Benefits

Improved stewardship to increase the health and survival of recently planted trees is one strategy for increasing cost-effectiveness. An evaluation of the Sacramento Shade program found that tree survival rates had a substantial impact on projected benefits (Hildebrandt et al. 1996). Higher survival rates increase energy savings and reduce tree removal and planting costs.

Work to increase survival rates

Conifers and broadleaf evergreens intercept rainfall and particulate matter year round as well as reduce windspeeds and provide shade, which lowers summer cooling and winter heating costs. Locating these types of trees in yards, parks, school grounds, and other open-space areas can increase benefits.

Target tree plantings with highest return

Energy benefits can be further increased by planting a higher percentage of trees in locations that produce the greatest energy savings, such as opposite west-facing walls and close to buildings with air conditioning. Keep in mind that evergreen trees should not be planted on the southern side of buildings because their branches and leaves block the warm rays of the winter sun. By customizing tree locations to increase numbers in high-yield sites, energy savings can be boosted.

Customize planting locations

45

Reducing Program Costs

Reduce up-front and establishment costs

Cost effectiveness is influenced by program costs as well as benefits:

Cost effectiveness = total benefit/total program cost

Cutting costs is one strategy to increase cost effectiveness. A substantial percentage of total program cost occurs during the first 5 years and is associated with tree planting and establishment (McPherson 1993). Some strategies to reduce these costs include:

- Plant bare-root or smaller tree stock.

- Use trained volunteers for planting and pruning of young trees (fig. 22).

- Provide followup care to increase tree survival and reduce replacement costs.

- Select and locate trees to avoid conflicts with infrastructure.

Use less expensive stock where appropriate

Where growing conditions are likely to be favorable, such as yard or garden settings, it may be cost effective to use smaller, less expensive stock or bare-root trees. In highly urbanized settings and sites subject to vandalism, however, large stock may survive the initial establishment period better than small stock.

Tree Trust

Figure 22—Trained volunteers can plant and maintain young trees, allowing the community to accomplish more at less cost and providing satisfaction for participants.

Although organizing and training volunteers requires labor and resources, it is usually less costly than contracting the work, and it can help build more support for your program. A cadre of trained volunteers can easily maintain trees until they reach a height of about 20 ft and limbs are too high to prune from the ground with pole pruners. By the time trees reach this size they are well established. Pruning during this establishment period should result in trees that will require less care in the long term. Training young trees can provide a strong branching structure that requires less frequent thinning and shaping (Costello 2000). Ideally, young trees should be inspected and pruned every other year for the first 5 years after planting.

As trees grow larger, pruning costs may increase on a per-tree basis. The frequency of pruning will influence these costs, as it takes longer to prune a tree that has not been pruned in 10 years than one that was pruned a few years ago. Although pruning frequency differs by species and location, a return frequency of about 5 to 8 years is usually sufficient for older trees (Miller 1997).

Investing in the resources needed to promote tree establishment during the first 5 years after planting is usually worthwhile, because once trees are established they have a high probability of continued survival. If your program has targeted trees on private property, then encourage residents to attend tree-care workshops. Develop standards of "establishment success" for different types of tree species. Perform periodic inspections to alert residents to tree health problems, and reward those whose trees meet your program's establishment standards. Replace dead trees as soon as possible, and identify ways to improve survivability.

Carefully select and locate trees to avoid conflicts with overhead power lines, sidewalks, and underground utilities. Time spent planning the planting will result in long-term savings. Also consider soil type and irrigation, microclimate, and the type of activities occurring around the tree that will influence its growth and management.

When evaluating the bottom line—trees pay us back—do not forget to consider benefits other than the stormwater-runoff reductions, energy savings, atmospheric CO_2 reductions, and other tangible benefits. The magnitude of benefits related to employment opportunities, job training, community building, reduced violence, and enhanced human health and well-being can be substantial (fig. 23). Moreover, these benefits extend beyond the site where trees are planted, furthering collaborative efforts to build better communities.

For more information on urban and community forestry program design and implementation, see the list of additional resources in appendix 1.

Prune early

Match tree to site

It all adds up—trees pay us back

Figure 23—Trees pay us back in tangible and intangible ways.

Brian Jorgenson

Chapter 5. General Guidelines for Selecting and Placing Trees

Guidelines for Energy Savings
Maximizing Energy Savings From Shading

The right tree in the right place can save energy and reduce tree care costs. In midsummer, the sun shines on the east side of a building in the morning, passes over the roof near midday, and then shines on the west side in the afternoon (see fig. 4). Electricity use is highest during the afternoon when temperatures are warmest and incoming sunshine is greatest. Therefore, the west side of a home is the most important side to shade (Sand 1993) (fig. 24).

Depending on building orientation and window placement, sun shining through windows can heat a home quickly during the morning hours. The east side is the second most important side to shade when considering the net impact of tree shade on energy savings (fig. 24). Deciduous trees on the east side provide summer shade and more winter solar heat gain than evergreens.

Trees located to shade south walls can block winter sunshine and increase heating costs because during winter the sun is lower in the sky and shines on the south side of homes (fig. 25). The warmth the sun provides is an asset, and planting evergreen trees on the southern side of a home would block southern exposures and solar collectors. Use solar-friendly trees to the south because the bare branches of these deciduous trees allow most sunlight to strike the building (some solar-unfriendly deciduous trees can reduce sunlight striking the south side of buildings by 50 percent even without leaves) (Ames 1987). Examples of solar-friendly trees include most species and cultivars of maples, crapemyrtle,

Where should shade trees be planted?

Figure 24—Locate trees to shade west and east windows (from Sand 1993).

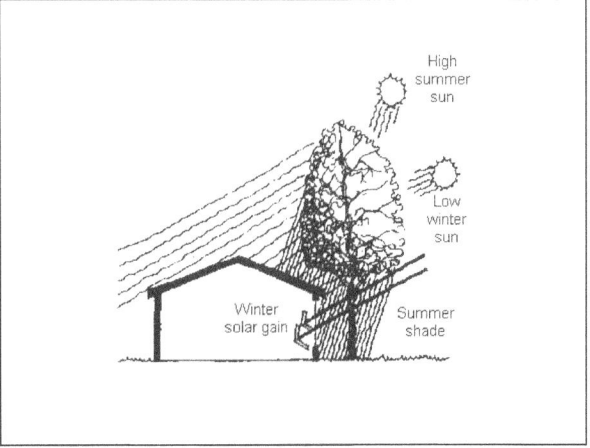

Figure 25—Select solar-friendly trees for southern exposures and locate them close enough to provide winter solar access and summer shade (from Sand 1991).

honeylocust, sweetgum, and zelkova (see "Common and Scientific Names" section). Some solar-unfriendly trees include most oaks, sycamore, most elms, and river birch (McPherson et al. 1994).

To maximize summer shade and minimize winter shade, locate shade trees about 10 to 20 ft south of the home. As trees grow taller, prune lower branches to allow more sun to reach the building if this will not weaken the tree's structure (fig. 26).

Although the closer a tree is to a home the more shade it provides, roots of trees that are too close can damage the foundation. Branches too close to the building can make it difficult to maintain exterior walls and windows. Keep trees 10 ft or farther from the home depending on mature crown spread, to avoid these conflicts. Trees within 30 to 50 ft of the home most effectively shade windows and walls.

Paved patios and driveways can become **heat sinks** that warm the home during the day. Shade trees can make them cooler and more comfortable spaces. If a home

Figure 26—Trees south of a home before and after pruning. Lower branches are pruned up to increase heat gain from winter sun (from Sand 1993).

is equipped with an air conditioner, shading can reduce its energy use, but do not plant vegetation so close that it will obstruct the flow of air around the unit.

Plant only small-growing trees under overhead power lines, and avoid planting directly above underground water and sewer lines if possible. Contact your local utility company before planting to determine where underground lines are located and which tree species should not be planted below power lines.

Planting Windbreaks for Heating Savings

A tree's size and crown density can make it ideal for blocking wind, thereby reducing the impacts of cold winter weather. Locate rows of trees perpendicular to the prevailing wind (fig. 27), usually the north and west side of homes in the Temperate Interior West region.

Design the windbreak row to be longer than the building being sheltered because windspeed increases at the edge of the windbreak. Ideally, the windbreak should be planted upwind about 25 to 50 ft from the building and should consist of dense evergreens that will grow to twice the height of the building they shelter (Heisler 1986, Sand 1991). Avoid planting windbreaks that will block sunlight to south and east walls (fig. 28). Trees should be spaced close enough to form a dense screen, but not so close that they will block sunlight to each other, causing lower branches to self-prune. Most conifers can be spaced about 6 ft on center. If there is room for two or more rows, then space rows 10 to 12 ft apart.

Plant dense evergreens

Evergreens are preferred over deciduous trees for windbreaks because they provide better wind protection. The ideal windbreak tree is fast growing, visually dense, has strong branch attachments, and has stiff branches that do not self-prune.

Figure 27—Evergreens protect a building from dust and cold by reducing windspeeds (from Sand 1993).

Figure 28—Midwinter shadows from a well-located windbreak and shade trees do not block solar radiation on the south-facing wall (from Sand 1993).

Your local cooperative extension agent or urban forester can help you select appropriate trees for your area.

In settings where vegetation is not a fire hazard, evergreens planted close to the home create airspaces that reduce air infiltration and heat loss. Allow shrubs to form thick hedges, especially along north, west, and east walls.

Selecting Trees to Maximize Benefits

The ideal shade tree has a fairly dense, round crown with limbs broad enough to partially shade the roof. Given the same placement, a large tree will provide more shade than a small tree. Deciduous trees allow sun to shine through leafless branches in winter. Plant small trees where nearby buildings or power lines limit aboveground space. Columnar trees are appropriate in narrow side yards. Because the best location for shade trees is relatively close to the west and east sides of buildings, the most suitable trees will be strong and capable of resisting storm damage, disease, and pests (Sand 1994). Examples of trees not to select for placement near buildings include cottonwoods and silver maple because of their invasive roots, weak wood, and large size, and ginkgos because of their sparse shade and slow growth.

Picking the right tree

When selecting trees, match the tree's water requirements with those of surrounding plants. For instance, select low-water-use species for planting in areas that receive little irrigation. Also, match the tree's maintenance requirements with the amount of care and the type of use different areas in the landscape receive. For instance, tree species that drop fruit that can be a slip-and-fall problem should not be planted near paved areas that are frequently used by pedestrians. Check with your local landscape professional before selecting trees to make sure that they are well suited to the site's soil and climatic conditions.

Use the following practices to plant and manage trees strategically to maximize energy conservation benefits:

Maximizing energy savings from trees

- Increase community-wide tree canopy, and target shade to streets, parking lots, and other paved surfaces, as well as air-conditioned buildings.

- Shade west- and east-facing windows and walls.

- Avoid planting trees to the south of buildings.

- Select solar-friendly trees opposite east- and south-facing walls.

- Shade air conditioners, but don't obstruct airflow.

- Avoid planting trees too close to utilities and buildings.

- Create multirow, evergreen windbreaks where space permits that are longer than the building.

Guidelines for Reducing Carbon Dioxide

Because trees in common areas and other public places may not shelter buildings from sun and wind and reduce energy use, carbon dioxide (CO_2) reductions are primarily due to sequestration. Fast-growing trees sequester more CO_2 initially than slow-growing trees, but this advantage can be lost if the fast-growing trees die at younger ages. Large trees have the capacity to store more CO_2 than smaller trees (fig. 29). To maximize CO_2 sequestration, select tree species that are well suited to the site where they will be planted. Consult with your local arborist to select the right tree for your site. Trees that are not well adapted will grow slowly, show symptoms of stress, or die at an early age. Unhealthy trees do little to reduce atmospheric CO_2 and can be unsightly liabilities in the landscape.

Design and management guidelines that can increase CO_2 reductions include the following:

- Maximize use of woody plants, especially trees, as they store more CO_2 than do herbaceous plants and grasses.

- Plant more trees where feasible, and immediately replace dead trees to compensate for CO_2 lost through removal.

- Create diverse habitats, with trees of different ages and species, to promote a continuous canopy cover over time.

(photo courtesy of Brian Jorgenson)

Brian Jorgenson

Figure 29—Compared with small trees, large trees can store more carbon, filter more air pollutants, intercept more rainfall, and provide greater energy savings. Here young white ash trees line a downtown Boise street.

- Group species with similar landscape maintenance requirements together and consider how irrigation, pruning, fertilization, weed, pest, and disease control can be minimized.

- Reduce CO_2 associated with landscape management by using push mowers (not gas or electric), hand saws (not chain saws), pruners (not gas/electric shears), rakes (not leaf blowers), and employ landscape professionals who don't have to travel far to your site.

- Reduce maintenance by reducing turfgrass and planting drought-tolerant or environmentally friendly landscapes.

- Consider the project's lifespan when selecting species. Fast-growing species will sequester more CO_2 initially than slow-growing species, but may not live as long.

- Provide ample space belowground for tree roots to grow so that they can maximize CO_2 sequestration and tree longevity.

- When trees die or are removed, salvage as much wood as possible for use as furniture and other long-lasting products to delay decomposition.

- Plant trees, shrubs, and vines in strategic locations to maximize summer shade and reduce winter shade, thereby reducing atmospheric CO_2 emissions associated with power production.

Guidelines for Reducing Stormwater Runoff

Trees are mini-reservoirs, controlling runoff at the source because their leaves and branch surfaces intercept and store rainfall, thereby reducing runoff volumes and erosion of water-courses, as well as delaying the onset of peak flows. Rainfall interception by large trees is a relatively inexpensive first line of defense in the battle to control nonpoint-source pollution.

When selecting trees to maximize rainfall interception benefits, consider the following:

- Select tree species with physiological features that maximize interception, such as evergreen foliage, large leaf surface area, and rough surfaces that store water (Metro 2002).

- Increase interception by planting large trees where possible (fig. 30).

- Plant trees that are in leaf when precipitation levels are highest.

- Plant low-water-use tree species where appropriate and native species that, once established, require little supplemental irrigation.

Figure 30—Trees can create a continuous canopy for maximum rainfall interception, even in commercial areas. In this example, a swale in the median filters runoff and provides ample space for large trees. Parking-space-sized planters contain the soil volume required to grow healthy, large trees (from Metro 2002).

- In bioretention areas, such as roadside swales, select species that tolerate inundation, are long-lived, wide-spreading, and fast-growing (Metro 2002).

- Do not pave over streetside planting strips for easier weed control; this can reduce tree health and increase runoff.

- Bioswales in parking lots and other paved areas store and filter stormwater while providing good conditions for trees.

Guidelines for Improving Air Quality Benefits

Trees, sometimes called the "lungs of our cities," are important because of their ability to remove contaminants from the air. The amount of gaseous pollutants and particulates removed by trees depends on their size and architecture, as well as local meteorology and pollutant concentrations.

Along streets, in parking lots, and in commercial areas, locate trees to maximize shade on paving and parked vehicles. Shade trees reduce heat that is stored or reflected by paved surfaces. By cooling streets and parking areas, trees reduce emissions of evaporative hydrocarbons from parked cars and thereby reduce smog formation (Scott et al. 1999). Large trees can shade a greater area than smaller trees, but should be used only where space permits. Remember that a tree needs space for both branches and roots. Keep in mind also that the soil along streets and parking lots will likely be compacted, and measures to reduce this problem, such as the use of engineered or structural soils, must be taken.

Tree planting and management guidelines to improve air quality include the following (Nowak 2000, Smith and Dochinger 1976):

- Select species that tolerate pollutants that are present in harmful concentrations. For example, in areas with high ozone (O_3) concentration avoid sensitive species such as white and green ash, tulip poplar, and Austrian pine (Noble et al. 1988).

- Conifers have high surface-to-volume ratios and retain their foliage year-round, which may make them more effective than deciduous species. In parking areas, however, species should be carefully chosen to avoid those that give off sticky residues.

- Species with long leaf stems (e.g., ash, maple) and hairy plant parts (e.g., oak, birch, sumac) are especially efficient interceptors.

- Effective uptake depends on proximity to the pollutant source and the amount of biomass. Where space and fire conditions permit, plant multilayered stands near the source of pollutants.

- In areas with unhealthy O_3 concentrations, maximize use of plants that emit low levels of biogenic volatile organic compounds to reduce O_3 formation.

- Sustain large, healthy trees; they produce the most benefits.

- To reduce emissions of volatile organic compounds and other pollutants, plant trees to shade parked cars and conserve energy.

Guidelines for Avoiding Conflicts With Infrastructure

Trees can become liabilities when they conflict with power lines, underground utilities, and other infrastructure elements. Guidelines to reduce conflicts with infrastructure include the following:

- Before planting, contact your local before-digging company, such as Call Before You Dig, Utility Notification Center, or One Call, to locate underground water, sewer, gas, and telecommunications lines.

- Avoid locating trees where they will block streetlights or views of traffic and commercial signs.

- Check with local transportation officials for sight visibility requirements. Keep trees at least 30 ft away from street intersections to ensure visibility.

- Avoid planting shallow-rooting species near sidewalks, curbs, and paving where tree roots can heave pavement if planted too close. Generally, avoid planting within 3 ft of pavement, and remember that trunk flare at the base of large trees can displace soil and paving for a considerable distance. Consider strategies to reduce damage by tree roots such as meandering sidewalks around trees (Costello and Jones 2003).

- Plant only small trees (<25 ft tall) under overhead power lines, and do not plant directly above underground water and sewer lines (fig. 31). Avoid locating trees where they will block illumination from streetlights or views of street signs in parking lots, commercial areas, and along streets.

Maintenance requirements and public safety concerns influence the type of trees selected for public places. The ideal public tree is not susceptible to wind

Figure 31—Know where power lines and other utility lines are before planting. Under power lines, use only small-growing trees ("low zone") and avoid planting directly above underground utilities. Larger trees may be planted where space permits ("medium" and "tall zones") (from ISA 1992).

damage and branch drop, does not require frequent pruning, produces negligible litter, is deep-rooted, has few serious pest and disease problems, and tolerates a wide range of soil conditions, irrigation regimes, and air pollutants. Because relatively few trees have all these traits, it is important to match the tree species to the planting site by determining what issues are most important on a case-by-case basis. For example, parking-lot trees should be tolerant of hot, dry conditions, have strong branch attachments, and be resistant to attacks by pests that leave vehicles covered with sticky exudates. Check with your local landscape professional for horticultural information on tree traits.

Guidelines for Maximizing Long-Term Benefits

Selecting a tree from the nursery that has a high probability of becoming a healthy, trouble-free mature tree is critical to a successful outcome. Therefore, select the very best stock at your nursery and, when necessary, reject nursery stock that does not meet industry standards.

The health of the tree's root ball is critical to its ultimate survival. If the tree is in a container, check for matted roots by sliding off the container. Roots should penetrate to the edge of the root ball, but not densely circle the inside of the container or grow through drain holes. As well, at least two large structural roots should emerge from the trunk within 1 to 3 in of the soil surface. If there are no roots in the upper portion of the root ball, it is undersized and the tree should not be planted.

Another way to evaluate the quality of the tree before planting is to gently move the trunk back and forth. A good tree trunk bends and does not move in the soil, whereas a poor trunk bends a little and pivots at or below the soil line—a tell-tale sign of a poorly anchored tree.

Planting trees correctly

Dig the planting hole 1 in shallower than the depth of the root ball to allow for some settling after watering. Make the hole two to three times as wide as the root ball and loosen the sides of the hole to make it easier for roots to penetrate. Place the tree so that the root flare is at the top of the soil. If the structural roots have grown properly as described above, the top of the root ball will be slightly higher (1 to 2 in) than the surrounding soil to allow for settling. Backfill with the native soil unless it is very rocky or sandy, in which case you may want to add composted organic matter such as peat moss or shredded bark (fig. 32).

Planting trees in urban plazas, commercial areas, and parking lots poses special challenges because of limited soil volume and poor soil structure. For trees to deliver benefits over the long term they require enough soil volume to grow and remain healthy. Matching tree species to the site's soil volume can reduce sidewalk and curb damage as well. Figure 33 shows recommended soil volumes for different

Figure 32— Prepare a broad planting area, plant the tree with the root flare at or just above ground level, and provide a berm/water ring to retain water (drawing courtesy of International Society of Arboriculture). (Note that trunk flare shown here represents a tree grown under optimum conditions. In trees grown under poorer conditions, the trunk flare may be hidden beneath the soil. These trees should be rejected in favor of those grown more carefully, or at the very least, the soil should be removed to expose the flare.)

sized trees. Engineered or structural soils can be placed under the hardscape to increase rooting space while meeting engineering requirements. For more information on structural soils see *Reducing Infrastructure Damage by Tree Roots: A Compendium of Strategies* (Costello and Jones 2003).

Use the extra soil left after planting to build a berm outside the root ball that is 6 in high and 3 ft in diameter. Soak the tree, and gently rock it to settle it in. Cover the basin with a 2- to 4-in layer of mulch, but avoid placing mulch against the tree trunk. Water the new tree two to three times a week and increase the amount of water as the tree grows larger. Generally, a tree requires about 1 in of water per week, although in areas of the Temperate Interior West trees may require as much as 2 in per week at the height of summer (Post 2007). A rain gauge or soil moisture sensor (tensiometer) can help determine tree watering needs, or contact your local cooperative extension agent or water conservancy district for recommendations.

After you've planted your tree, remember the following:

• Inspect your tree several times a year, and contact a local landscape professional if problems develop.

• If your tree needed staking to keep it upright, remove the stake and ties after

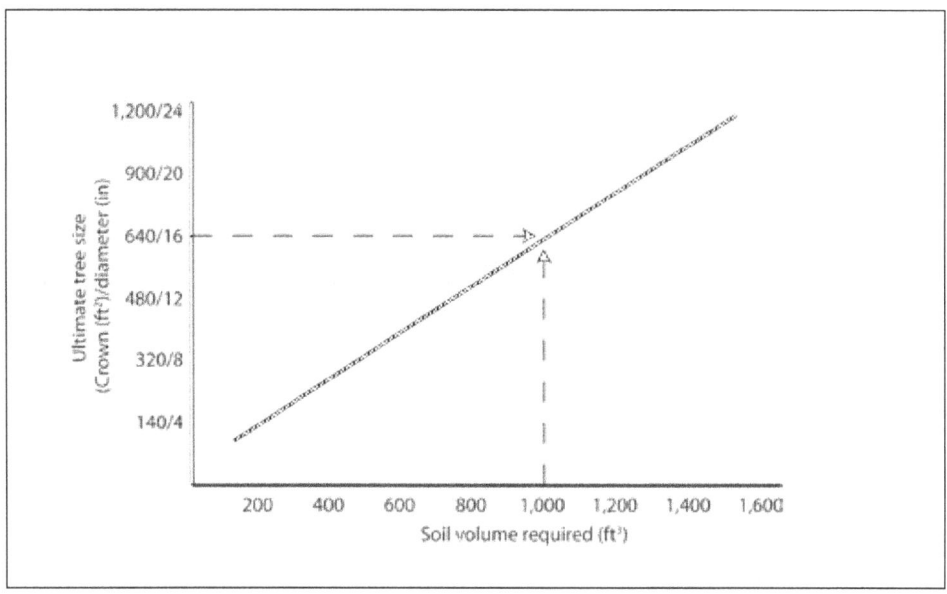

Figure 33—Developed from several sources by Urban (1992), this graph shows the relationship between tree size and required soil volume. For example, a tree with a 16-inch diameter at breast height (41 cm) with 640 ft^2 of crown projection area (59.5 m^2 under the dripline) requires 1,000 ft^3 (28 m^3) of soil (from Costello and Jones 2003)

1 year or as soon as the tree can hold itself up. The staking should allow some tree movement, as this movement sends hormones to the roots causing them to grow and create greater tree stability. It also promotes trunk taper and growth.

- Reapply mulch and irrigate the tree as needed.

- Leave lower side branches on young trees for the first year and prune back to 4 to 6 in to accelerate tree diameter development. Remove these lateral branches after the first full year. Prune the young tree to maintain a central main trunk and equally spaced branches. For more information, see Costello (2000) and Gilman (2002). As the tree matures, have it pruned on a regular basis by a certified arborist or other experienced professional.

- By keeping your tree healthy, you maximize its ability to produce shade, intercept rainfall, reduce atmospheric CO_2, and provide other benefits.

For more information on tree selection, planting, establishment, and care see the resources listed in appendix 1.

Glossary of Terms

annual fuel utilization efficiency (AFUE)—A measure of space heating equipment efficiency defined as the fraction of energy output per energy input.

anthropogenic—Produced by humans.

biodiversity—The variety of life forms in a given area. Diversity can be categorized in terms of the number of species, the variety in the area's plant and animal communities, the genetic variability of the animals or plants, or a combination of these elements.

biogenic—Produced by living organisms.

biogenic volatile organic compounds (BVOCs)—Hydrocarbon compounds from vegetation (e.g., isoprene, monoterpene) that exist in the ambient air and contribute to the formation of smog or may themselves be toxic. Emission rates ($\mu g \cdot g^{-1} \cdot hr^{-1}$) used for this report follow Benjamin and Winer (1998):

- *Fraxinus americana*—0.0 (isoprene); 0.0 (monoterpene)
- *Acer platanoides*—0.0 (isoprene); 2.8 (monoterpene)
- *Malus* spp.—0.0 (isoprene); 0.1 (monoterpene)
- *Picea pungens*—4.0 (isoprene); 1.1 (monoterpene)

canopy—A layer or multiple layers of branches and foliage at the top or crown of a forest's trees.

canopy cover—The area of land surface that is covered by tree canopy, as seen from above.

Ccf—One hundred cubic feet.

climate—The average weather for a particular region and period (usually 30 years). Weather describes the short-term state of the atmosphere; climate is the average pattern of weather for a particular region. Climatic elements include precipitation, temperature, humidity, sunshine, wind velocity, phenomena such as fog, frost, and hailstorms, and other measures of weather.

climate effects—Impact on residential space heating and cooling (kg of CO_2 per tree per year) from trees located more than 50 ft from a building owing to associated reductions in windspeeds and summer air temperatures.

community forests—The sum of all woody and associated vegetation in and around human settlements, ranging from small rural villages to metropolitan regions.

contract rate—The percentage of residential trees cared for by commercial arborists; the proportion of trees for which a specific service (e.g., pruning or pest management) is contracted.

control costs—The marginal cost of preventing, controlling, or mitigating an impact.

crown—The branches and foliage at the top of a tree.

cultivar (derived from "cultivated variety")—Denotes certain cultivated plants that are clearly distinguishable from others by any characteristic, and that when reproduced (sexually or asexually), retain their distinguishing characteristics. In the United States, "variety" is often considered synonymous with "cultivar."

damage costs—The total estimated economic loss produced by an impact.

deciduous—Trees or shrubs that lose their leaves every fall.

diameter at breast height (d.b.h.)—The diameter of a tree outside the bark measured 4.5 ft above the ground on the uphill side (where applicable) of the tree.

dripline—The area beneath a tree marked by the outer edges of the branches.

emission factor—The rate of CO_2, nitrogen dioxide (NO_2), sulfur dioxide (SO_2), and small particulate matter (PM_{10}) output resulting from the consumption of electricity, natural gas, or any other fuel source.

evapotranspiration (ET)—The total loss of water by evaporation from the soil surface and by transpiration from plants, from a given area, and during a specified period.

evergreens—Trees or shrubs that are never entirely leafless. Evergreens may be broadleaved or coniferous (cone-bearing with needlelike leaves).

greenspace—Urban trees, forests, and associated vegetation in and around human settlements, ranging from small communities in rural settings to metropolitan regions.

hardscape—Paving and other impervious ground surfaces that reduce infiltration of water into the soil.

heat sinks—Paving, buildings, and other surfaces that store heat energy from the sun.

hourly pollutant dry deposition—Removal of gases from the atmosphere by direct transfer to natural surfaces and absorption of gases and particles by natural surfaces such as vegetation, soil, water, or snow.

interception—Amount of rainfall held on tree leaves and stem surfaces.

kWh (kilowatt-hour)—A unit of work or energy, measured as 1 kW (1000 watts) of power expended for 1 hour.

leaf area index (LAI)—Total leaf area per unit area of crown if crown were projected in two dimensions.

leaf surface area (LSA)—Measurement of area of one side of a leaf or leaves.

mature tree—A tree that has reached a desired size or age for its intended use. Size, age, and economic maturity differ depending on the species, location, growing conditions, and intended use.

mature tree size—The approximate size of a tree 40 years after planting.

metric tonne—A measure of weight (abbreviated "t") equal to 1 000 000 grams (1000 kilograms) or 2,205 pounds.

municipal forester—A person who manages public street or park trees (municipal forestry programs) for the benefit of the community.

MWh (megawatt-hour)—A unit of work or energy, measured as 1 megawatt (1 000 000 watts) of power expended for 1 hour. One MWh is equivalent to 3.412 MBtu.

nitrogen oxides (oxides of nitrogen, NOx)—A general term for compounds of nitric acid (NO), nitrogen dioxide (NO_2), and other oxides of nitrogen. Nitrogen oxides are typically created during combustion processes and are major contributors to smog formation and acid deposition. NO_2 may cause numerous adverse human health effects.

ozone (O_3)—A strong-smelling, pale blue, reactive toxic chemical gas with molecules of three oxygen atoms. It is a product of the photochemical process involving the Sun's energy. Ozone exists in the upper layer of the atmosphere as well as at the Earth's surface. Ozone at the Earth's surface can cause numerous adverse human health effects. It is a major component of smog.

peak flow (or peak runoff)—The maximum rate of runoff at a given point or from a given area, during a specific period.

photosynthesis—The process in green plants of converting water and CO_2 into sugar by using light energy; accompanied by the production of oxygen.

PM_{10} (particulate matter)—Major class of air pollutants consisting of tiny solid or liquid particles of soot, dust, smoke, fumes, and mists. The size of the particles

(10 microns or smaller, about 0.0004 in or less) allows them to enter the air sacs (gas-exchange region) deep in the lungs where they may be deposited and cause adverse health effects. PM_{10} also reduces visibility.

reduced power plant emissions—Reduced emissions of carbon dioxide (CO_2) or other pollutants that result from reductions in building energy use owing to the moderating effect of trees on climate. Reduced energy use for heating and cooling results in reduced demand for electrical energy, which translates into fewer emissions by power plants.

resource unit (RU)—The value used to determine and calculate benefits and costs of individual trees. For example, the amount of air conditioning energy saved in kWh/year per tree, air-pollutant uptake in pounds per year per tree, or rainfall intercepted in gallons per tree per year.

riparian habitats—Narrow strips of land bordering creeks, rivers, lakes, or other bodies of water.

seasonal energy efficiency ratio (SEER)—Ratio of cooling output to power consumption; kBtu-output/kWh-input as a fraction. It is the Btu of cooling output during normal annual usage divided by the total electric energy input in kilowatt-hours during the same period.

sequestration—Annual net rate that a tree removes CO_2 from the atmosphere through the processes of photosynthesis and respiration (kg of CO_2 per tree per year).

shade coefficient—The percentage of light striking a tree crown that is transmitted through gaps in the crown. This is the percentage of light that hits the ground.

shade effects—Impact on residential space heating and cooling (kg of CO_2 per tree per year) from trees located within 50 ft of a building.

solar-friendly trees—Trees that have characteristics that reduce blocking of winter sunlight. According to one numerical ranking system, these traits include open crowns during the winter heating season, leaves that fall early and appear late, relatively small size, and a slow growth rate (Ames 1987).

stem flow—Amount of rainfall that travels down the tree trunk and onto the ground.

sulfur dioxide (SO_2)—A strong-smelling, colorless gas that is formed by the combustion of fossil fuels. Power plants, which may use coal or oil high in sulfur content, can be major sources of SO_2. Sulfur oxides contribute to the problem of acid deposition.

t—See metric tonne.

therm—A unit of heat equal to 100,000 British thermal units (BTUs) or 100 kBtu.

throughfall—Amount of rainfall that falls directly to the ground below the tree crown or drips onto the ground from branches and leaves.

transpiration—The loss of water vapor through the stomata of leaves.

tree or canopy cover—Within a specific area, the percentage covered by the crown of an individual tree or delimited by the vertical projection of its outermost perimeter; small openings in the crown are ignored. Used to express the relative importance of individual species within a vegetation community or to express the coverage of woody species.

tree litter—Fruit, leaves, twigs, and other debris shed by trees.

tree-related CO_2 emissions—CO_2 released when growing, planting, and caring for trees.

tree surface saturation storage capacity—The maximum volume of water that can be stored on a tree's leaves, stems, and bark. This part of rainfall stored on the canopy surface does not contribute to surface runoff during and after a rainfall event.

urban heat island—An area in a city where summertime air temperatures are 3 to 8 °F warmer than temperatures in the surrounding countryside. Urban areas are warmer for two reasons: (1) dark construction materials for roofs and asphalt absorb solar energy, and (2) few trees, shrubs, or other vegetation provide shade and cool the air.

volatile organic compounds (VOCs)—Hydrocarbon compounds that exist in the ambient air. VOCs contribute to the formation of smog or are themselves toxic. VOCs often have an odor. Some examples of VOCs are gasoline, alcohol, and the solvents used in paints.

willingness to pay—The maximum amount of money an individual would be willing to pay for nonmarket, public goods and services provided by environmental amenities such as trees and forests rather than do without.

Common and Scientific Names

Common name	Scientific name
Plants:	
American linden	*Tilia americana* L.
American sycamore	*Platanus occidentalis* L.
Ash	*Fraxinus* spp.
Austrian pine	*Pinus nigra* J.F. Arnold
Birch	*Betula* spp.
Blackgum	*Nyssa* spp.
Black locust	*Robinia pseudoacacia* L.
Black oak	*Quercus velutina* Lam.
Black walnut	*Juglans nigra* L.
Blue spruce	*Picea pungens* Engelm.
Callery pear	*Pyrus calleryana* Dcne.
Cottonwood	*Populus* spp.
Crabapple	*Malus* spp.
Crapemyrtle	*Lagerstroemia indica* L.
English elm	*Ulmus procera* Salisb.
Elm	*Ulmus* spp.
Ginkgo	*Ginkgo biloba* L.
Green ash	*Fraxinus pennsylvanica* Marshall
Hawthorn	*Crataegus* spp.
Honeylocust	*Gleditsia triacanthos* L.
London planetree	*Platanus hybrida* Brot.
Maple	*Acer* spp.
Northern catalpa	*Catalpa speciosa*
Northern red oak	*Quercus rubra* L.
Norway maple	*Acer platanoides* L.
Oak	*Quercus* spp.
Poplar	*Populus* spp.
River birch	*Betula nigra* L.
Russian olive	*Elaeagnus angustifolia* L.
Scotch pine	*Pinus sylvestris* L.
Siberian elm	*Ulmus pumila* L.
Silver maple	*Acer saccharinum* L.
Sugar maple	*Acer saccharum* Marsh.
Sumac	*Rhus* spp.
Sweetgum	*Liquidambar styraciflua* L.
Sycamore	*Platanus* spp.
Tree of heaven	*Ailanthus altissima* (P. Mill.) Swingle
Tulip poplar	*Liriodendron tulipifera* L.
White ash	*Fraxinus americana* L.
Zelkova	*Zelkova serrata* (Thunb.) Makino
Insects:	
Emerald ash borer	*Agrilus planipennis* Fairmaire

Metric Equivalents

When you know:	Multiply by:	To find:
Inches (in)	25,400	Microns
Inches (in)	25.4	Millimeters (mm)
Inches (in)	2.54	Centimeters (cm)
Feet (ft)	.305	Meters (m)
Square feet (ft^2)	.0929	Square meters (m^2)
Miles (mi)	1.61	Kilometers (km)
Square miles (mi^2)	2.59	Square kilometers (km^2)
Acre-feet	1233.6	Cubic meters (m^3)
Gallons (gal)	.00378	Cubic meters (m^3)
Ounces	28.35	Grams (g)
Ounces	28,349,523	Micrograms (μg)
Pounds (lb)	.454	Kilograms (kg)
Pounds per square foot (lb/ft^2)	4.882	Kilograms per square meter (kg/m^2)
Tons (ton)	.907	Metric tonne (t)
Million BTUs	.2931	Megawatt hours (MWh)
Therms	29.31	Kilowatt hours (kWh)
Fahrenheit (°F)	.56 (F-32)	Celsius (°C)

Acknowledgments

A number of people assisted with data collection and provided technical assistance: Brian Jorgenson, Jerry Stallsmith (Community Forestry, Boise, Idaho); Eric Wing (Information Technology Department, Boise, Idaho); Johanna Bell (Public Works Department, Boise, Idaho); Stephanie Huang, Christine Yang, and Aywon-Anh Nguyen (Center for Urban Forest Research).

Tree care expenditure information was provided by Brian Jorgenson (City of Boise, Idaho), Michael Bowman (City of Lewiston, Idaho), Earl Moran (City of Nampa, Idaho), John Franks (City of Payette, Idaho), Paul Nelson (City of Caldwell, Idaho), Janet Davis and Ezekiel Willard (Idaho Tree Preservation), Mary Jane Fields (DG Turf Farm & Nursery), Kevin Allen (Pro Care Landscape Services), and Eddie Brock (The Lawn Company Maintenance).

Dr. John Lloyd (University of Idaho), Dick Post (University of Nevada Cooperative Extension), Dave Stephenson (Idaho Department of Lands, Urban and Community Forestry Coordinator), and Susan Stead (Nevada Department of Conservation and Natural Resources, Division of Forestry) provided helpful reviews of this work.

Mark Buscaino, Keith Cline, and Barbara Hollenbeck (U.S. Department of Agriculture, Forest Service, State and Private Forestry); Susan Stead (Nevada Department of Conservation and Natural Resources, Division of Forestry); and Dave Stephenson (Idaho Department of Lands, Urban and Community Forestry Coordinator) provided invaluable support for this project.

References

Agrimet. 2006. Pacific Northwest Cooperative Agricultural Weather Network. Historical dayfile data access. http://www.usbr.gov/pn/agrimet/webaghrread. html. (30 March 2006).

Akbari, H.; Davis, S.; Dorsano, S.; Huang, J.; Winnett, S., eds. 1992. Cooling our communities: a guidebook on tree planting and light-colored surfacing. Washington, DC: U.S. Department of the Interior, Environmental Protection Agency. 26 p.

Alliance for Community Trees. 2006. Tree by tree, street by street. http://actrees. org. (27 January 2007).

American Forests. 2001. Regional ecosystem analysis for the Willamette/Lower Columbia region of northwestern Oregon and southwestern Washington State. Calculating the value of nature. Washington, DC: American Forests. 16 p.

American Forests. 2004. Urban Ecological Analysis, Montgomery, AL. Washington, DC. 12 p.

Ames, M.J. 1987. Solar friendly trees report. Portland, OR: City of Portland Energy Office. [Pages unknown].

Anderson, L.M.; Cordell, H.K. 1988. Residential property values improve by landscaping with trees. Southern Journal of Applied Forestry. 9: 162–166.

Bedker, P.J.; O'Brien, J.G.; Mielke, M.E. 1995. How to prune trees. NA-FR-01-95. [Newtown Square, PA]: U.S. Department of Agriculture, Forest Service, Northeastern Area State and Private Forestry. 28 p.

Bell, J. 2006. Personal communication. Stormwater management costs. Stormwater Program Coordinator, Public Works Department, City of Boise, P.O. Box 500, Boise, ID 83701-0500.

Benjamin, M.T.; Winer, A.M. 1998. Estimating the ozone-forming potential of urban trees and shrubs. Atmospheric Environment. 32: 53–68.

Bernhardt, E.; Swiecki, T.J. 1993. The state of urban forestry in California: results of the 1992 California urban forest survey. Sacramento: California Department of Forestry and Fire Protection. 51 p.

Brandle, J.R.; Nickerson, H.D.; 1996. Windbreaks for snow management. EC96-1770-X. Lincoln, NE: University of Nebraska Extension. [Pages unknown.]

Bratkovich, S.M. 2001. Utilizing municipal trees: ideas from across the country. NA-TP-06-01. Newtown Square, PA: U.S. Department of Agriculture, Forest Service, Northeastern Area State and Private Forestry. 91 p.

Brenzel, K.N., ed. 2001. Sunset western garden book. 7th ed. Menlo Park, CA: Sunset Books, Inc. 768 p.

Brock J.H. 1998. Invasion, ecology and management of *Elaeagnus angustifolia* (Russian olive) in the Southwestern U.S.A. In: Starfinger, U.; Edwards, K.; Kowarik, I.; Williamson, M., eds. Plant invasions: ecological mechanisms and human responses. Leiden, The Netherlands: Backhuys Publishers. 372 p.

Cappiella, K.; Schueler, T.; Wright, T. 2005. Urban watershed forestry manual. Ellicott City, MD: Center for Watershed Protection. 138 p.

Cardelino, C.A.; Chameides, W.L. 1990. Natural hydrocarbons, urbanization, and urban ozone. Journal of Geophysical Research. 95(9): 13971–13979.

Chameides W.L.; Lindsay, R.W.; Richardson, J.; Kiang, C.S. 1988. The role of biogenic hydrocarbons in urban photochemical smog: Atlanta as a case study. Science. 241: 1473–1475.

Chicago Climate Exchange. 2007. About CCX. http://www.chicagoclimatex.com/about/index.html. (21 January 2007).

CO2e.com. 2007. CO_2e market size and pricing. http://www.co2e.com/strategies/AdditionalInfo.asp?PageID=273#1613. (21 January 2007).

Cook, D.I. 1978. Trees, solid barriers, and combinations: alternatives for noise control. In: Proceedings of the National Urban Forestry Conference. ESF Pub. 80-003. Syracuse, NY: State University of New York: 330–334.

Costello, L.R. 2000. Training young trees for structure and form. [Video] V99-A. Oakland, CA: University of California, Agriculture and Natural Resources, Communication Services Cooperative Extension Service.

Costello, L.R.; Jones, K.S. 2003. Reducing infrastructure damage by tree roots: a compendium of strategies. Cohasset, CA: Western Chapter of the International Society of Arboriculture. 119 p.

Dwyer, J.F.; McPherson, E.G.; Schroeder, H.W.; Rowntree, R.A. 1992. Assessing the benefits and costs of the urban forest. Journal of Arboriculture. 18(5): 227–234.

Dwyer, M.C.; Miller, R.W. 1999. Using GIS to assess urban tree canopy benefits and surrounding greenspace distributions. Journal of Arboriculture. 25(2): 102–107.

European Climate Exchange. 2006. Historic data—ECX CFI futures contract. http://www.europeanclimateexchange.com. (29 August 2006).

Fazio, J.R. [N.d.]. Tree City USA Bulletin Series. Lincoln, NE: The National Arbor Day Foundation.

Geiger, J. 2001. Save dollars with shade. Davis, CA: U.S. Department of Agriculture, Forest Service, Pacific Southwest Research Station. 4 p. http://www.fs.fed.us/psw/programs/cufr/products/3/cufr_149.pdf. (25 January 2007).

Geiger, J. 2002a. Green plants or power plants? Davis, CA: U.S. Department of Agriculture, Forest Service, Pacific Southwest Research Station. 4 p. http://www.fs.fed.us/psw/programs/cufr/products/3/cufr_148.pdf. (25 January 2007).

Geiger, J. 2002b. Where are all the cool parking lots? Davis, CA: U.S. Department of Agriculture, Forest Service, Pacific Southwest Research Station. 4 p. http://www.fs.fed.us/psw/programs/cufr/products/3/cufr_151.pdf. (25 January 2007).

Geiger, J. 2003. Is all your rain going down the drain? Davis, CA: U.S. Department of Agriculture, Forest Service, Pacific Southwest Research Station. 4 p. http://www.fs.fed.us/psw/programs/cufr/products/cufr_392_rain_down_the_drain.pdf. (25 January 2007).

Geiger, J. 2006. Trees—the air pollution solution. Davis, CA: U.S. Department of Agriculture, Forest Service, Pacific Southwest Research Station. 4 p. http://www.fs.fed.us/psw/programs/cufr/products/3/ cufr_658_Air_pollution_solution.pdf. (25 January 2007).

Gilman, E.F. 1997. Trees for urban and suburban planting. Albany, NY: Delmar Publishing. 688 p.

Gilman, E.F. 2002. An illustrated guide to pruning. 2nd ed. Albany, NY: Delmar Publishing. 256 p.

Gonzalez, S. 2004. Personal communication. Assistant maintenance superintendent, City of Vallejo, 111 Amador St., Vallejo, CA 94590.

Grant, R.H.; Heisler, G.M.; Goa, W. 2002. Estimation of pedestrian level UV exposure under trees. Photochemistry and Photobiology. 75(4): 369–376.

Guenther, A.B.; Monson, R.K.; Fall, R. 1991. Isoprene and monoterpene emission rate variability: observations with eucalyptus and emission rate algorithm development. Journal of Geophysical Research. 96: 10799–10808.

Guenther, A.B.; Zimmermann, P.R.; Harley, P.C.; Monson, R.K.; Fall, R. 1993. Isoprene and monoterpene emission rate variability: model evaluations and sensitivity analyses. Journal of Geophysical Research. 98: 12609–12617.

Hammer, T.T.; Coughlin, R.; Horn, E. 1974. The effect of a large urban park on real estate value. Journal of the American Institute of Planning. July: 274–275.

Hammond J.; Zanetto, J.; Adams, C. 1980. Planning solar neighborhoods. Sacramento, CA: California Energy Commission. 179 p.

Hargrave, R.; Johnson, G.R.; Zins, M.E. 2002. Planting trees and shrubs for long-term health. MI-07681-S. St. Paul, MN: University of Minnesota Extension Service. 12 p.

Harris, R.W.; Clark, J.R.; Matheny, N.P. 2003. Arboriculture. 4th ed. Englewood Cliffs, NJ: Regents/Prentice Hall. 592 p.

Hauer, R.J.; Hruska, M.C.; Dawson, J.O. 1994. Trees and ice storms: the development of ice storm-resistant urban tree populations. Special Publ. 94-1. Urbana, IL: Department of Forestry, University of Illinois at Urbana-Champaign. 12 p.

Haugen, L.M. 1998. How to identify and manage Dutch elm disease. NA-PR-07-98. [Newtown Square, PA]: U.S. Department of Agriculture, Forest Service, Northeastern Area State and Private Forestry. 26 p.

Heisler, G.M. 1986. Energy savings with trees. Journal of Arboriculture. 12(5): 113–125.

Hightshoe, G.L. 1988. Native trees, shrubs, and vines for urban and rural America. New York: Van Nostrand Reinhold. 832 p.

Hildebrandt, E.W.; Kallett, R.; Sarkovich, M.; Sequest, R. 1996. Maximizing the energy benefits of urban forestation. In: Proceedings of the ACEEE 1996 summer study on energy efficiency in buildings. Washington, DC: American Council for an Energy Efficient Economy: 121–131. Vol. 9.

Hudson, B. 1983. Private sector business analogies applied in urban forestry. Journal of Arboriculture. 9(10): 253–258.

Hull, R.B. 1992. How the public values urban forests. Journal of Arboriculture. 18(2): 98–101.

Hunter, J. 2000. *Ailanthus altissima* (Miller) Swingle. In: Bossard, C.C.; Randall, J.M.; Hoshovsky, M.C., eds. Invasive plants of California's wildlands. Berkeley: University of California Press, Berkeley: 32–36.

Idaho Power Company. 2006. Schedule 1. Residential service electricity rates. http://www.idahopower.com/aboutus/regulatoryinfo/tariffPdf.asp?id=156&.pdf. (15 March 2006).

Intergovernmental Panel on Climate Change [IPCC]. 2001. Technical summary. Climate change 2001: the scientific basis. Geneva. 63 p.

Intermountain Gas Company. 2006. Prices. RS-1 Residential service. http://www.intgas.com/aboutbilling/prices.html. (15 March 2006).

International Society of Arboriculture [ISA]. 1992. Avoiding tree and utility conflicts. Savoy, IL. 4 p.

International Society of Arboriculture. 2006. Welcome to the International Society of Arboriculture. http://www.isa-arbor.com/home.aspx. (27 January 2007).

Jo, H.K.; McPherson, E.G. 1995. Carbon storage and flux in residential greenspace. Journal of Environmental Management. 45: 109–133.

Jorgenson, B. 2006. Personal communication. City forester, Boise Parks and Recreation Department, Community Forestry Unit, 4969 Dorman St., Boise, ID, 83705.

Kaplan, R. 1992. Urban forestry and the workplace. In: Gobster, P.H., ed. Managing urban and high-use recreation settings. Gen. Tech. Rep. NC-163. St. Paul, MN: U.S. Department of Agriculture, Forest Service, North Central Research Station:41–45.

Kaplan, R.; Kaplan, S. 1989. The experience of nature: a psychological perspective. Cambridge, United Kingdom: Cambridge University Press. 360 p.

Kim, S.; Byun, D.W.; Cheng, F.-Y.; Czader, B.; Stetson, S.; Nowak, D.; Walton, J.; Estes, M.; Hitchcock, D. 2005. Modeling effects of land use land cover changes on meteorology and air quality in Houston, Texas, over the last two decades. In: Proceedings of the 2005 Atmospheric Sciences Air Quality Conference. [Place of publication unknown]. Available at: http://ams.confex.com/ams/pdfpapers/92244.pdf. (23 January 2007).

Lewis, C.A. 1996. Green nature/human nature: the meaning of plants in our lives. Chicago: University of Illinois Press. 176 p.

Luley, C.J.; Bond, J. 2002. A plan to integrate management of urban trees into air quality planning. Naples, NY: Davey Resource Group. 61 p.

Maco, S.E.; McPherson, E.G. 2003. A practical approach to assessing structure, function, and value of street tree populations in small communities. Journal of Arboriculture. 29(2): 84–97.

Marion, W.; Urban, K. 1995. User's manual for TMY2s—typical meteorological years. Golden, CO: National Renewable Energy Laboratory. 49 p.

Markwardt, L.J. 1930. Comparative strength properties of woods grown in the United States. Tech. Bull. 158. Washington, DC: U.S. Department of Agriculture. 38 p.

McHale, M. 2003. Carbon credit markets: Is there a role for community forestry? In: Kollin, C., ed. 2003 national urban forest conference proceedings. Washington, DC: American Forests: 74–77.

McKenzie, D.; Gedalof, Z.; Peterson, D.L.; Mote, P. 2004. Climate change, wildfire, and conservation. Conservation Biology. 18(4): 890–902.

McPherson, E.G. 1984. Planting design for solar control. In: McPherson, E.G., ed. Energy-conserving site design. Washington, DC: American Society of Landscape Architects: 141–164. Chapter 8.

McPherson, E.G. 1992. Accounting for benefits and costs of urban greenspace. Landscape and Urban Planning. 22: 41–51.

McPherson, E.G. 1993. Evaluating the cost effectiveness of shade trees for demand-side management. The Electricity Journal. 6(9): 57–65.

McPherson, E.G. 1995. Net benefits of healthy and productive forests. In: Bradley, G.A., ed. Urban forest landscapes: integrating multidisciplinary perspectives. Seattle, WA: University of Washington Press: 180–194.

McPherson, E.G. 2000. Expenditures associated with conflicts between street tree root growth and hardscape in California. Journal of Arboriculture. 26(6): 289–297.

McPherson, E.G. 2001. Sacramento's parking lot shading ordinance: environmental and economic costs of compliance. Landscape and Urban Planning. 57: 105–123.

McPherson, E.G.; Mathis, S., eds. 1999. Proceedings of the Best of the West summit. Sacramento, CA: Western Chapter, International Society of Arboriculture. 93 p.

McPherson, E.G.; Muchnick, J. 2005. Effects of tree shade on asphalt concrete pavement performance. Journal of Arboriculture. 31(6): 303–309.

McPherson, E.G.; Nowak, D.J.; Heisler, G.; Grimmond, S.; Souch, C.; Grant, R.; Rowntree, R.A. 1997. Quantifying urban forest structure, function, and value: Chicago's Urban Forest Climate Project. Urban Ecosystems. 1: 49–61.

McPherson, E.G.; Nowak, D.J.; Rowntree, R.A. 1994. Chicago's urban forest ecosystem: results of the Chicago Urban Forest Climate Project. Gen. Tech. Rep. NE-186. Radnor [Newtown Square], PA: U.S. Department of Agriculture, Forest Service, Northeastern Research Station. 201 p.

McPherson, E.G.; Peper, P.J. 1995. Infrastructure repair costs associated with street trees in 15 cities. In: Watson, G.W.; Neely, D., eds. Trees and building sites. Champaign, IL: International Society of Arboriculture: 49–63.

McPherson, E.G.; Sacamano, P.L.; Wensman, S. 1993. Modeling benefits and costs of community tree plantings. Albany, CA: U.S. Department of Agriculture, Forest Service, Pacific Southwest Research Station. 170 p.

McPherson, E.G.; Simpson, J.R. 1999. Carbon dioxide reduction through urban forestry: guidelines for professional and volunteer tree planters. Gen. Tech. Rep. PSW-171. Albany, CA: U.S. Department of Agriculture, Forest Service, Pacific Southwest Research Station. 237 p.

McPherson, E.G., Simpson, J.R. 2002. A comparison of municipal forest benefits and costs in Modesto and Santa Monica, CA, USA. Urban Forestry and Urban Greening. 1: 61–74.

McPherson, E.G.; Simpson, J.R. 2003. Potential energy savings in buildings by an urban tree planting programme in California. Urban Forestry and Urban Greening. 2(2): 73–86.

McPherson, E.G.; Simpson, J.R.; Peper, P.J.; Gardner, S.L.; Vargas, K.E.; Maco, S.E.; Xiao, Q. 2006a. Coastal Plain community tree guide: benefits, costs, and strategic planting. Gen Tech. Rep. PSW-GTR-201. Albany, CA: U.S. Department of Agriculture, Forest Service, Pacific Southwest Research Station. 99 p.

McPherson, E.G.; Simpson, J.R.; Peper, P.J.; Gardner, S.L.; Vargas, K.E.; Maco, S.E.; Xiao, Q. 2006b. Piedmont community tree guide: benefits, costs, and strategic planting. Gen Tech. Rep. PSW-GTR-200. Albany, CA: U.S. Department of Agriculture, Forest Service, Pacific Southwest Research Station. 95 p.

McPherson, E.G.; Simpson, J.R.; Peper, P.J.; Gardner, S.L.; Vargas, K.E.; Xiao, Q. [In press]. Northeast community tree guide: benefits, costs, and strategic planting. Gen Tech. Rep. PSW-GTR-202. Albany, CA: U.S. Department of Agriculture, Forest Service, Pacific Southwest Research Station. 102 p.

McPherson, E.G.; Simpson, J.R.; Peper, P.J.; Maco, S.E.; Gardner, S.L.; Cozad, S.K.; Xiao, Q. 2006c. Midwest community tree guide: benefits, costs, and strategic planting. Gen. Tech. Rep. PSW-GTR-199. Albany, CA: U.S. Department of Agriculture, Forest Service, Pacific Southwest Research Station. 85 p.

McPherson, E.G.; Simpson, J.R.; Peper, P.J.; Maco, S.E.; Xiao, Q.; Hoefer, P.J. 2003. Northern mountain and prairie community tree guide: benefits, costs, and strategic planting. Albany, CA: U.S. Department of Agriculture, Forest Service, Pacific Southwest Research Station. 88 p.

McPherson, E.G.; Simpson, J.R.; Peper, P.J.; Maco, S.E.; Xiao, Q.; Mulrean, E. 2004. Desert Southwest community tree guide: benefits, costs, and strategic planting. Albany, CA: U.S. Department of Agriculture, Forest Service, Pacific Southwest Research Station. 65 p.

McPherson, E.G.; Simpson, J.R.; Peper, P.J.; Scott, K.; Xiao, Q. 2000. Tree guidelines for coastal southern California communities. Sacramento, CA: Local Government Commission. 97 p.

McPherson, E.G.; Simpson, J.R.; Peper, P.J.; Xiao, Q. 1999a. Benefit-cost analysis of Modesto's municipal urban forest. Journal of Arboriculture. 25(5): 235–248.

McPherson, E.G.; Simpson, J.R.; Peper, P.J.; Xiao, Q. 1999b. Tree guidelines for San Joaquin Valley communities. Sacramento, CA: Local Government Commission. 63 p.

Metro. 2002. Green streets: innovative solutions for stormwater and stream crossings. Portland, OR: Metro. 144 p.

Miller, R.W. 1997. Urban forestry: planning and managing urban greenspaces. 2d ed. Upper Saddle River, NJ: Prentice-Hall. 502 p.

More, T.A.; Stevens, T.; Allen, P.G. 1988. Valuation of urban parks. Landscape and Urban Planning. 15: 139–152.

Morgan, R. [N.d.]. An introductory guide to community and urban forestry in Washington, Oregon, and California. Portland, OR: World Forestry Center. 25 p.

Morgan, R. 1993. A technical guide to urban and community forestry. Portland, OR: World Forestry Center. 49 p.

National Arbor Day Foundation. 2006. Color your world. http://www.arborday. org. (27 January 2007).

Neely, D., ed. 1988. Valuation of landscape trees, shrubs, and other plants. 7th ed. Urbana, IL: International Society of Arboriculture. 50 p.

Noble, R.D.; Martin, J.L.; Jensen, K.F., eds. 1988. Air pollution effects on vegetation, including forest ecosystems. Proceedings of the second US–USSR symposium. Gov. Doc. A13.42/2:2:A:7. Broomall [Newtown Square], PA: U.S. Department of Agriculture, Forest Service, Northeastern Research Station. 311 p.

Nowak, D.J. 1994. Air pollution removal by Chicago's urban forest. In: McPherson, E.G.; Nowak, D.J.; Rowntree, R.A., eds. Chicago's urban forest ecosystem: results of the Chicago urban forest climate project. Gen. Tech. Rep. NE-186. Radnor [Newtown Square], PA: U.S. Department of Agriculture, Forest Service, Northeastern Research Station: 63–82.

Nowak, D.J. 2000. Tree species selection, design, and management to improve air quality. In: Scheu, D.L., ed. 2000 ASLA annual meeting proceedings. Washington, DC: American Society of Landscape Architects: 23–27.

Nowak, D.J.; Civerolo, K.L.; Rao, S.T.; Sistla, G.; Luley, C.J.; Crane, D.E. 2000. A modeling study of the impact of urban trees on ozone. Atmospheric Environment. 34: 1601–1613.

Nowak, D.J.; Crane, D.E. 2002. Carbon storage and sequestration by urban trees in the USA. Environmental Pollution. 116: 381–389.

Ottinger, R.L.; Wooley, D.R.; Robinson, N.A.; Hodas, D.R.; Babb, S.E. 1990. Environmental costs of electricity. New York: Oceana Publications. 769 p.

Parsons, R.; Tassinary, L.G.; Ulrich, R.S.; Hebl, M.R.; Grossman-Alexander, M. 1998. The view from the road: implications for stress recovery and immunization. Journal of Environmental Psychology. 18(2): 113–140.

Pearce, D 2003. The social cost of carbon and its policy implications. Oxford Review of Public Policy. 19(3): 362–384.

Peper, P.J.; McPherson, E.G. 2003. Evaluation of four methods for estimating leaf area of isolated trees. Urban Forestry and Urban Greening. 2(1): 19–29.

Peper, P.J.; McPherson, E.G.; Simpson, J.R.; Gardner, S.L.; Vargas, K.E. [In press]. City of Boise, Idaho, Municipal Forest Resource Analysis. Internal

Tech. Rep. Davis, CA: U.S. Department of Agriculture, Forest Service, Pacific Southwest Research Station, Center for Urban Forest Research.

Pillsbury, N.H.; Reimer, J.L.; Thompson, R.P. 1998. Tree volume equations for fifteen urban species in California. Tech. Rep. 7. San Luis Obispo, CA: Urban Forest Ecosystems Institute, California Polytechnic State University. 56 p.

Platt, R.H.; Rowntree, R.A.; Muick, P.C., eds. 1994. The ecological city. Boston, MA: University of Massachusetts. 292 p.

Pokorny, J.D. 2003. Urban tree risk management: a community guide to program design and implementation. NA-TP-03-03. Newtown Square, PA: U.S. Department of Agriculture, Forest Service, Northeastern Area State and Private Forestry. [Pages unknown].

Post, R. 2007. Personal communication. Former Western Area Director, University of Nevada Cooperative Extension, Reno, NV [no current address available].

Ramsay, S. 2002. Personal communication. Executive Director, Trees Forever, 770 7th Ave., Marion, IA 52302.

Richards, N.A.; Mallette, J.R.; Simpson, R.J.; Macie, E.A. 1984. Residential greenspace and vegetation in a mature city: Syracuse, New York. Urban Ecology. 8: 99–125.

Rosenzweig, C.; Solecki, W.; Parshall, L.; Hodges, S. 2006. Mitigating New York City's heat island with urban forestry, living roofs, and light surfaces. New York City regional heat island initiative final report 06-06. Albany, NY: New York State Energy Research and Development Authority. 173 p.

Sand, M. 1991. Planting for energy conservation in the North. Minneapolis, MN: Minnesota Department of Natural Resources. 19 p.

Sand, M. 1993. Energy saving landscapes: the Minnesota homeowner's guide. Minneapolis, MN: Minnesota Department of Natural Resources. [Pages unknown].

Sand, M. 1994. Design and species selection to reduce urban heat island and conserve energy. In: Proceedings from the sixth national urban forest conference: growing greener communities. Washington, DC: American Forests. 282 p.

Schroeder, H.W.; Cannon, W.N. 1983. The esthetic contribution of trees to residential streets in Ohio towns. Journal of Arboriculture. 9: 237–243.

Schroeder, T. 1982. The relationship of local park and recreation services to residential property values. Journal of Leisure Research. 14: 223–234.

Scott, K.I.; McPherson, E.G.; Simpson, J.R. 1998. Air pollutant uptake by Sacramento's urban forest. Journal of Arboriculture. 24(4): 224–234.

Scott, K.I.; Simpson, J.R.; McPherson, E.G. 1999. Effects of tree cover on parking lot micro-climate and vehicle emissions. Journal of Arboriculture. 25(3): 129–142.

Simpson, J.R. 1998. Urban forest impacts on regional space conditioning energy use: Sacramento County case study. Journal of Arboriculture. 24(4): 201-214.

Smith, W.H. 1990. Air pollution and forests. New York: Springer-Verlag. 618 p.

Smith, W.H.; Dochinger, L.S. 1976. Capability of metropolitan trees to reduce atmospheric contaminants. In: Santamour, F.S.; Gerhold, H.D.; Little, S., eds. Better trees for metropolitan landscapes. Gen. Tech. Rep. NE-22. Upper Darby [Newtown Square], PA: U.S. Department of Agriculture, Forest Service, Northeastern Research Station: 49–60.

Sullivan, W.C.; Kuo, E.E. 1996. Do trees strengthen urban communities, reduce domestic violence? Arborist News. 5(2): 33–34.

Summit, J.; McPherson, E.G. 1998. Residential tree planting and care: a study of attitudes and behavior in Sacramento, California. Journal of Arboriculture. 24(2): 89–97.

Sydnor, T.D.; Gamstetter, D.; Nichols, J.; Bishop, B.; Favorite, J.; Blazer, C.; Turpin, L. 2000. Trees are not the root of sidewalk problems. Journal of Arboriculture. 26:20–29.

Taha, H. 1996. Modeling impacts of increased urban vegetation on ozone air quality in the South Coast Air Basin. Atmospheric Environment. 30: 3423–3430.

Tellman, B. 1997. Exotic pest plant introduction in the American Southwest. Desert Plants. 13(1): 3–10.

Thompson, R.P.; Ahern, J.J. 2000. The state of urban and community forestry in California. San Luis Obispo, CA: Urban Forest Ecosystems Institute, California Polytechnic State University. 48 p.

Treelink. 2007. Improving urban and community forests by providing Internet-based information, tools, and inspiration. http://www.treelink.org. (29 June 2007).

Tretheway, R.; Manthe, A. 1999. Skin cancer prevention: another good reason to plant trees. In: McPherson, E.G.; Mathis, S. Proceedings of the Best of the West summit. Davis, CA: University of California: 72–75.

Tschantz, B.A.; Sacamano, P.L. 1994. Municipal tree management in the United States. Kent, OH: Davey Resource Group. 71 p.

Tyrvainen, L. 1999. Monetary valuation of urban forest amenities in Finland. Res. Pap. 739. Vantaa, Finland: Finnish Forest Research Institute. 129 p.

Ulrich, R.S. 1985. Human responses to vegetation and landscapes. Landscape and Urban Planning. 13: 29–44.

Urban, J. 1992. Bringing order to the technical dysfunction within the urban forest. Journal of Arboriculture. 18(2): 85–90.

Urban Horticulture Institute. 2003. Recommended urban trees: site assessment and tree selection for stress tolerance. http://www.hort.cornell.edu/UHI/outreach/recurbtree/index.html. (7 February 2007).

U.S. Census Bureau. 2006. State and county quick facts. http://quickfacts.census.gov/qfd/index.html. (March 2006).

U.S. Department of Agriculture, Forest Service [USDA FS]. 2006a. i-Tree: tools for assessing and managing community forests. http://www.itreetools.org. (27 January 2007).

U.S. Department of Agriculture, Forest Service [USDA FS]. 2006b. Urban tree cover and air quality planning. http://www.treescleanair.org. (21 January 2007).

U.S. Department of Agriculture, Natural Resource Conservation Service, Agroforestry Center [USDA NRCS Agroforesty Center]. 2005. Working trees for treating waste. Western Arborist. 31: 50–52.

U.S. Department of Agriculture, Soil Conservation Service [USDA SCS]. 1986. Urban hydrology for small watersheds. Technical Release 55. 2nd ed. Washington, DC. 164 p.

U.S. Department of Transportation. 1995. Highway traffic noise analysis and abatement policy and guidance. Washington, DC: Federal Highway Administration. 67 p.

U.S. Environmental Protection Agency [US EPA]. 1998. Ap-42 Compilation of air pollutant emission factors. 5th ed. Research Triangle Park, NC. Volume I. [Pages unknown.]

U.S. Environmental Protection Agency [US EPA]. 2003. E-GRID (E-GRID2002 Edition). http://www.epa.gov/cleanenergy/egrid/index.htm. (6 December 2006).

U.S. Environmental Protection Agency [U.S. EPA]. 2006. Green book: nonattainment areas for criteria pollutants. http://www.epa.gov/air/oaqps/ greenbk/index.html. (6 December 2006).

van Rentergehm, T.; Botteldooren, D.; Cornelis, W.M.; Gabriels, D.; 2002. Reducing screen-induced refraction of noise barriers in wind by vegetative screens. Acta Acustica United with Acustica. 88: 231–238.

Vargas, K.E.; McPherson, E.G.; Simpson J.R.; Peper, P.J.; Gardner, S.L.; Xiao, Q. 2006. City of Albuquerque, New Mexico, municipal forest resource analysis. Internal Tech. Rep. Davis, CA: U.S. Department of Agriculture, Forest Service, Pacific Southwest Research Station, Center for Urban Forest Research. 51 p.

Vargas, K.E.; McPherson, E.G.; Simpson J.R.; Peper, P.J.; Gardner, S.L.; Xiao, Q. [In press]. Interior West community tree guide: benefits, costs, and strategic planting. Gen Tech. Rep. PSW-GTR-205. Albany, CA: U.S. Department of Agriculture, Forest Service, Pacific Southwest Research Station.

Wang, M.Q.; Santini, D.J. 1995. Monetary values of air pollutant emissions in various U.S. regions. Transportation Research Record 1475: 33–41.

Watson, G.W.; Himelick, E.B. 1997. Principles and practice of planting trees and shrubs. Savoy, IL: International Society of Arboriculture. 199 p.

Wing, E. 2006. Personal communication. Boise GIS databases. GIS Programmer Analyst, GIS Division, Public Works Department, City of Boise, P.O. Box 500, Boise, ID 83701.

Wolf, K.L. 1999. Nature and commerce: human ecology in business districts. In: Kollin, C., ed. Building cities of green: proceedings of the 1999 national urban forest conference. Washington, DC: American Forests: 56–59.

Xiao, Q.; McPherson, E.G. 2002. Rainfall interception by Santa Monica's municipal urban forest. Urban Ecosystems. 6: 291–302.

Xiao, Q.; McPherson, E.G.; Simpson, J.R.; Ustin, S.L. 1998. Rainfall interception by Sacramento's urban forest. Journal of Arboriculture. 24(4): 235–244.

Xiao, Q.; McPherson, E.G.; Simpson, J.R.; Ustin, S.L. 2000. Winter rainfall interception by two mature open grown trees in Davis, California. Hydrological Processes. 14(4): 763–784.

Appendix 1: Additional Resources

Additional information regarding urban and community forestry program design and implementation can be obtained from the following sources:

Utilizing Municipal Trees: Ideas From Across the Country by S.M. Bratkovich

Urban Forestry: Planning and Managing Urban Greenspaces by R.W. Miller

An Introductory Guide to Community and Urban Forestry in Washington, Oregon, and California by N.R. Morgan

A Technical Guide to Urban and Community Forestry by N.R. Morgan

Urban Tree Risk Management: A Community Guide to Program Design and Implementation edited by J.D. Pokorny

For additional information on tree selection, planting, establishment, and care see the following resources:

Alliance for Community Trees: http://actrees.org

How to Prune Trees by P.J. Bedker, J.G. O'Brien, and M.E. Mielke

Training Young Trees for Structure and Form, a video by L.R. Costello

An Illustrated Guide to Pruning by E.F. Gilman

Planting Trees and Shrubs for Long-Term Health by R. Hargrave, G.R. Johnson, and M.E. Zins

Arboriculture, 4th ed., by R.W. Harris, J.R. Clark, and N.P. Matheny

Trees and Ice Storms: The Development of Ice Storm-Resistant Urban Tree Populations, by R.J. Hauer, M.C. Hruska, and J.O. Dawson

How to Identify and Manage Dutch Elm Disease by L.M. Haugen

Native Trees, Shrubs, and Vines for Urban and Rural America by G.L. Hightshoe

International Society of Arboriculture: http://www.isa-arbor.com, including their Tree City USA Bulletin series by J.R. Fazio

National Arbor Day Foundation: http://www.arborday.org

TreeLink: http://www.treelink.org

Trees for Urban and Suburban Landscapes by E.F. Gilman

The Urban Horticulture Institute: http://www.hort.cornell.edu/UHI/outreach/ recurbtree/index.html

Principles and Practice of Planting Trees and Shrubs by G.W. Watson and E.B. Himelick

These suggested references are only a starting point. Your local cooperative extension agent, urban forester, or state forestry agency can provide you with up-to-date and local information.

Appendix 2: Benefit–Cost Information Tables

Information in this appendix can be used to estimate benefits and costs associated with proposed tree plantings. The tables contain data for representative small (crabapple), medium (Norway maple), and large (white ash) deciduous trees and a representative conifer (blue spruce) (see "Common and Scientific Names" section). Data are presented as annual values for each 5-year interval after planting (tables 6 to 17). Annual values incorporate effects of tree loss. Based on the results of our survey, we assume that 43.1 percent of the trees planted die by the end of the 40-year period.

For the benefits tables (tables 6, 9, 12, 15), there are two columns for each 5-year interval. In the first column, values describe resource units (RUs): for example, the amount of air conditioning energy saved in kilowatt hours per year per tree, air pollutant uptake in pounds per year per tree, and rainfall intercepted in gallons per year per tree. Energy and CO_2 benefits for residential yard trees are broken out by tree location to show how shading effects differ among trees opposite west-, south-, and east-facing building walls. The second column for each 5-year interval contains dollar values obtained by multiplying RUs by local prices (e.g., kWh saved [RU] × $/kWh).

In the costs tables (tables 7, 10, 13, 16), costs are broken down into categories for yard and public trees. Costs for yard trees do not differ by planting location (i.e., east, west, south walls). Although tree purchase and planting costs occur at year 1, we divided this value by 5 years to derive an average annual cost for the first 5-year period. All other costs are the estimated values for each year and not values averaged over 5 years.

Total net benefits are calculated by subtracting total costs from total benefits and are presented in tables 8, 11, 14, and 17. Data are presented for a yard tree opposite west-, south-, and east-facing walls, as well as for the public tree.

The last column in each table presents 40-year-average annual values. These numbers were calculated by dividing the total costs and benefits by 40 years.

Table 6—Annual benefits at 5-year intervals and 40-year average for a representative small tree (crabapple)

Benefits/tree	Year 5 RU	Year 5 Value (Dollars)	Year 10 RU	Year 10 Value (Dollars)	Year 15 RU	Year 15 Value (Dollars)	Year 20 RU	Year 20 Value (Dollars)	Year 25 RU	Year 25 Value (Dollars)	Year 30 RU	Year 30 Value (Dollars)	Year 35 RU	Year 35 Value (Dollars)	Year 40 RU	Year 40 Value (Dollars)	40-year average RU	40-year average Value (Dollars)
Cooling (kWh):																		
Yard: west	8	0.65	56	4.61	120	9.87	179	14.68	224	18.38	263	21.54	283	23.19	296	24.29	179	14.65
Yard: south	6	0.51	37	2.99	73	5.99	107	8.81	138	11.29	163	13.40	180	14.78	193	15.83	112	9.20
Yard: east	7	0.53	40	3.29	84	6.85	124	10.15	156	12.80	184	15.07	201	16.50	214	17.55	126	10.34
Public	6	0.51	36	2.94	69	5.67	99	8.15	124	10.13	144	11.82	158	12.92	168	13.74	100	8.23
Heating (therms):																		
Yard: west	0.58	0.67	2.77	3.23	4.70	5.48	6.26	7.30	7.08	8.26	7.76	9.06	7.94	9.26	7.96	9.29	5.63	6.57
Yard: south	0.59	0.69	2.67	3.12	4.17	4.87	5.28	6.16	5.65	6.59	5.94	6.92	5.89	6.88	5.76	6.73	4.49	5.24
Yard: east	0.55	0.64	2.42	2.82	3.92	4.57	5.11	5.96	5.72	6.67	6.22	7.25	6.37	7.44	6.42	7.49	4.59	5.36
Public	0.61	0.71	3.09	3.61	5.48	6.39	7.47	8.72	8.66	10.10	9.66	11.27	10.04	11.72	10.23	11.94	6.91	8.06
Net energy (kWh):																		
Yard: west	25	1.33	137	7.84	258	15.34	362	21.98	432	26.64	490	30.60	515	32.45	530	33.58	344	21.22
Yard: south	24	1.20	115	6.11	195	10.86	262	14.98	303	17.88	337	20.33	353	21.66	362	22.56	244	14.45
Yard: east	23	1.17	111	6.11	198	11.42	274	16.11	324	19.47	366	22.32	388	23.93	402	25.05	261	15.70
Public	24	1.22	127	6.55	230	12.06	318	16.87	377	20.24	427	23.09	452	24.63	467	25.68	303	16.29
Net carbon dioxide (lb):																		
Yard: west	16	0.05	90	0.30	180	0.60	260	0.87	319	1.07	371	1.24	399	1.33	420	1.40	257	0.86
Yard: south	15	0.05	75	0.25	138	0.46	196	0.65	238	0.79	275	0.92	298	1.00	317	1.06	194	0.65
Yard: east	15	0.05	74	0.25	143	0.48	206	0.69	252	0.84	294	0.98	320	1.07	340	1.14	205	0.69
Public	15	0.05	79	0.26	151	0.50	215	0.72	262	0.88	305	1.02	330	1.10	350	1.17	214	0.71
Air pollution (lb)[a]																		
Ozone uptake	0.010	0.01	0.058	0.03	0.117	0.06	0.178	0.09	0.234	0.12	0.289	0.15	0.338	0.17	0.386	0.20	0.20	0.10
Nitrogen dioxide uptake + avoided	0.020	0.01	0.117	0.06	0.229	0.12	0.331	0.17	0.409	0.21	0.476	0.24	0.516	0.26	0.546	0.28	0.33	0.17
Sulfur dioxide uptake + avoided	0.034	0	0.216	0.01	0.443	0.03	0.652	0.04	0.820	0.05	0.964	0.06	1.051	0.06	1.114	0.07	0.66	0.04
Small particulate matter uptake + avoided	0.007	0.01	0.046	0.04	0.107	0.10	0.180	0.17	0.246	0.23	0.259	0.24	0.266	0.24	0.271	0.25	0.17	0.16
Volatile organic compounds avoided	0.003	0	0.020	0	0.040	0.01	0.058	0.01	0.073	0.01	0.086	0.01	0.093	0.01	0.098	0.01	0.06	0.01
Biogenic volatile organic compounds released	0	0	-0.001	0	-0.002	0	-0.004	0	-0.005	0	-0.005	0	-0.005	0	-0.005	0	0	0
Total air pollution avoided + net uptake	0.074	0.02	0.456	0.15	0.934	0.31	1.395	0.47	1.777	0.61	2.069	0.70	2.259	0.76	2.410	0.80	1.42	0.48
Hydrology (gal)																		
Rainfall interception	8	0.04	47	0.23	94	0.47	142	0.71	187	0.93	231	1.16	271	1.35	309	1.55	161	0.81
Aesthetics and other:																		
Yard		4.07		9.41		12.19		12.60		11.44		9.36		6.80		4.05		8.74
Public		4.54		10.51		13.62		14.07		12.78		10.45		7.59		4.53		9.76
Total benefits:																		
Yard: west		5.51		17.93		28.91		36.63		40.70		43.05		42.68		41.39		32.10
Yard: south		5.38		16.15		24.29		29.41		31.66		32.46		31.56		30.02		25.12
Yard: east		5.35		16.14		24.87		30.58		33.30		34.52		33.90		32.59		26.41
Public		5.87		17.70		26.96		32.85		35.44		36.41		35.44		33.73		28.05

Note: Annual values incorporate effects of tree loss. We assume that 13 percent of trees planted die during the first 5 years and 30 1 percent during the remaining 35 years for a total mortality of 43 1 percent. RU = resource unit.

[a] Values are the same for yard and public trees.

Table 7—Annual costs (dollars per tree) at 5-year intervals and 40-year average for a representative small tree (crabapple)

Costs	Year 5	Year 10	Year 15	Year 20	Year 25	Year 30	Year 35	Year 40	40-year average
					Dollars				
Tree and planting[a]:									
Yard	35.00								4.38
Public	28.00								3.50
Pruning:									
Yard	0.23	0.17	0.16	2.30	2.22	2.15	2.07	2.00	1.21
Public	5.44	6.20	5.88	5.56	5.24	4.92	4.60	4.28	5.42
Remove and dispose:									
Yard	0.08	0.82	1.35	1.87	2.36	2.83	3.28	3.71	1.85
Public	0.26	0.98	1.61	2.23	2.81	3.38	3.91	4.42	2.22
Pest and disease									
Yard	0.03	0.07	0.11	0.15	0.18	0.21	0.23	0.26	0.14
Public	0.02	0.06	0.10	0.13	0.15	0.17	0.18	0.19	0.11
Infrastructure repair:									
Yard	0.04	0.10	0.15	0.21	0.25	0.29	0.33	0.36	0.20
Public	0.26	0.68	1.07	1.40	1.66	1.87	2.03	2.13	1.28
Irrigation:									
Yard	0	0	0	0	0	0	0	0	0
Public	1.34	0	0	0	0	0	0	0	0.18
Cleanup:									
Yard	0.01	0.03	0.04	0.06	0.07	0.08	0.10	0.10	0.06
Public	0.08	0.20	0.31	0.41	0.48	0.55	0.59	0.62	0.37
Liability and legal:									
Yard	0	0	0	0.01	0.01	0.01	0.01	0.01	0.01
Public	0.01	0.02	0.03	0.04	0.05	0.06	0.06	0.07	0.04
Admin./inspect/other:									
Yard	0	0	0	0	0	0	0	0	0
Public	0.52	1.34	2.10	2.74	3.26	3.67	3.98	4.18	2.51
Total costs:									
Yard	35.38	1.18	1.83	4.58	5.10	5.57	6.02	6.43	7.84
Public	35.93	9.49	11.10	12.50	13.66	14.61	15.35	15.89	15.64

Note: Annual values incorporate effects of tree loss. We assume that 13 percent of trees planted die during the first 5 years and 30.1 percent during the remaining 35 years for a total mortality of 43.1 percent.

[a]Although tree and planting costs occur in year 1, this value was divided by 5 years to derive an average annual cost for the first 5-year period.

Table 8—Annual net benefits (dollars per tree) at 5-year intervals and 40-year average for a representative small tree (crabapple)

Total net benefits	Year 5	Year 10	Year 15	Year 20	Year 25	Year 30	Year 35	Year 40	40-year average
					Dollars				
Yard: west	-30	17	27	32	36	37	37	35	24
Yard: south	-30	15	22	25	27	27	26	24	17
Yard: east	-30	15	23	26	28	29	28	26	19
Public	-30	8	16	20	22	22	20	18	12

Note: Annual values incorporate effects of tree loss. We assume that 13 percent of trees planted die during the first 5 years and 30.1 percent during the remaining 35 years for a total mortality of 43.1 percent. See table 6 for annual benefits and table 7 for annual costs.

Table 9—Annual benefits (dollars per tree) at 5-year intervals and 40-year average for a representative medium tree (Norway maple)

Benefits/tree	Year 5 RU	Year 5 Value	Year 10 RU	Year 10 Value	Year 15 RU	Year 15 Value	Year 20 RU	Year 20 Value	Year 25 RU	Year 25 Value	Year 30 RU	Year 30 Value	Year 35 RU	Year 35 Value	Year 40 RU	Year 40 Value	40-year average RU	40-year average Value
		Dollars		Dollars		Dollars		Dollars		Dollars		Dollars		Dollars		Dollars		Dollars
Cooling (kWh):																		
Yard: west	61	5.03	160	13.12	256	20.99	329	26.97	381	31.24	417	34.16	433	35.55	445	36.45	310	25.44
Yard: south	27	2.18	79	6.49	134	11.00	195	16.00	240	19.66	279	22.84	303	24.85	322	26.39	197	16.18
Yard: east	35	2.85	99	8.12	164	13.45	225	18.45	269	22.07	303	24.82	321	26.36	335	27.48	219	17.95
Public	25	2.01	68	5.58	112	9.17	159	13.06	194	15.89	224	18.35	243	19.89	257	21.06	160	13.12
Heating (therms):																		
Yard: west	1.44	1.68	3.65	4.26	5.66	6.60	6.99	8.16	7.93	9.25	8.34	9.73	8.39	9.79	8.37	9.76	6.35	7.40
Yard: south	0.48	0.56	0.71	0.83	0.69	0.80	0.78	0.90	0.83	0.97	0.92	1.07	0.98	1.14	1.02	1.20	0.80	0.93
Yard: east	0.87	1.01	2.42	2.82	3.88	4.53	5.15	6.00	6.05	7.06	6.57	7.66	6.76	7.88	6.86	8.01	4.82	5.62
Public	2.12	2.47	5.34	6.23	8.33	9.72	10.46	12.20	11.97	13.96	12.74	14.87	12.95	15.11	13.03	15.20	9.62	11.22
Net energy (kWh):																		
Yard: west	103	6.71	267	17.38	422	27.60	534	35.13	613	40.49	661	43.89	679	45.34	690	46.21	496	32.84
Yard: south	41	2.74	100	7.32	154	11.80	218	16.91	264	20.64	305	23.92	332	25.99	352	27.58	221	17.11
Yard: east	60	3.86	170	10.94	278	17.98	376	24.45	447	29.13	495	32.49	520	34.25	536	35.49	360	23.57
Public	87	4.48	224	11.80	356	18.88	466	25.26	545	29.85	597	33.22	622	35.00	639	36.25	442	24.34
Net carbon dioxide (lb):																		
Yard: west	82	0.27	205	0.68	323	1.08	412	1.38	478	1.59	516	1.72	532	1.78	543	1.81	386	1.29
Yard: south	45	0.15	110	0.37	174	0.58	239	0.80	289	0.96	326	1.09	348	1.16	365	1.22	237	0.79
Yard: east	55	0.18	145	0.48	234	0.78	313	1.04	372	1.24	410	1.37	429	1.43	443	1.48	300	1.00
Public	62	0.21	156	0.52	247	0.83	326	1.09	385	1.29	424	1.42	443	1.48	458	1.53	313	1.04
Air pollution (lb)[a]:																		
Ozone uptake	0.035	0.02	0.108	0.06	0.187	0.10	0.279	0.14	0.359	0.18	0.442	0.23	0.513	0.26	0.584	0.30	0.31	0.16
Nitrogen dioxide uptake + avoided	0.089	0.05	0.242	0.12	0.394	0.20	0.534	0.27	0.637	0.32	0.717	0.37	0.764	0.39	0.799	0.41	0.52	0.27
Sulfur dioxide uptake + avoided	0.188	0.01	0.519	0.03	0.851	0.05	1.161	0.07	1.386	0.08	1.562	0.09	1.663	0.10	1.737	0.10	1.13	0.07
Small particulate matter uptake + avoided	0.019	0.02	0.068	0.06	0.144	0.13	0.246	0.23	0.344	0.32	0.438	0.40	0.447	0.41	0.453	0.42	0.27	0.25
Volatile organic compounds avoided	0.017	0	0.046	0.01	0.075	0.01	0.101	0.01	0.121	0.02	0.136	0.02	0.145	0.02	0.151	0.02	0.10	0.01
Biogenic volatile organic compounds released	-0.002	0	-0.026	0	-0.075	-0.01	-0.142	-0.02	-0.213	-0.03	-0.286	-0.04	-0.286	-0.04	-0.286	-0.04	-0.16	-0.02
Total air pollution avoided + net uptake	0.345	0.09	0.956	0.27	1.576	0.48	2.180	0.71	2.634	0.89	3.009	1.07	3.245	1.14	3.438	1.21	2.17	0.73
Hydrology (gal):																		
Rainfall interception	101	0.50	308	1.54	532	2.66	796	3.98	1,023	5.12	1,259	6.30	1,461	7.30	1,663	8.31	893	4.46
Aesthetics and other:																		
Yard		23.22		20.33		18.50		16.68		14.88		13.13		11.43		9.81		16.00
Public		25.94		22.71		20.66		18.63		16.62		14.66		12.77		10.96		17.87
Total benefits:																		
Yard: west		30.80		40.21		50.32		57.87		62.98		66.10		67.00		67.36		55.33
Yard: south		26.71		29.83		34.02		39.07		42.49		45.50		47.03		48.13		39.10
Yard: east		27.87		33.57		40.41		46.86		51.27		54.35		55.56		56.30		45.77
Public		31.23		36.85		43.52		49.66		53.78		56.66		57.70		58.26		48.46

Note: Annual values incorporate effects of tree loss. We assume that 13 percent of trees planted die during the first 5 years and 30.1 percent during the remaining 35 years for a total mortality of 43.1 percent. RU = resource unit.

[a] Values are the same for yard and public trees.

Table 10—Annual costs (dollars per tree) at 5-year intervals and 40-year average for a representative medium tree (Norway maple)

Costs	Year 5	Year 10	Year 15	Year 20	Year 25	Year 30	Year 35	Year 40	40-year average
					Dollars				
Tree and planting[a]:									
Yard	35.00								4.38
Public	28.00								3.50
Pruning:									
Yard	0.23	2.45	2.37	2.30	2.22	6.13	5.91	5.70	3.40
Public	5.44	6.20	5.88	5.56	5.24	8.20	7.66	7.12	6.52
Remove and dispose:									
Yard	0.27	1.23	1.79	2.31	2.80	3.25	3.66	4.03	2.22
Public	2.29	1.46	2.13	2.75	3.33	3.87	4.36	4.80	2.72
Pest and disease									
Yard	0.05	0.10	0.15	0.18	0.21	0.24	0.26	0.28	0.17
Public	0.05	0.09	0.13	0.15	0.18	0.19	0.20	0.21	0.14
Infrastructure repair:									
Yard	0.08	0.14	0.20	0.25	0.30	0.33	0.31	0.39	0.24
Public	0.55	1.02	1.41	1.73	1.97	2.14	2.26	2.32	1.57
Irrigation:									
Yard	0	0	0	0	0	0	0	0	0
Public	1.34	0	0	0	0	0	0	0	0.18
Cleanup:									
Yard	0.02	0.04	0.06	0.07	0.09	0.10	0.09	0.11	0.07
Public	0.16	0.30	0.41	0.50	0.57	0.62	0.66	0.68	0.46
Liability and legal:									
Yard	0	0	0.01	0.01	0.01	0.01	0.01	0.01	0.01
Public	0.02	0.03	0.04	0.05	0.06	0.07	0.07	0.07	0.05
Admin./inspect/other:									
Yard	0	0	0	0	0	0	0	0	0
Public	1.09	2.01	2.77	3.39	3.86	4.21	4.43	4.54	3.07
Total costs:									
Yard	35.66	3.97	4.57	5.12	5.62	10.06	10.25	10.52	10.48
Public	38.94	11.12	12.78	14.14	15.21	19.30	19.64	19.75	18.21

Note: Annual values incorporate effects of tree loss. We assume that 13 percent of trees planted die during the first 5 years and 30.1 percent during the remaining 35 years for a total mortality of 43.1 percent.

[a]Although tree and planting costs occur in year 1, this value was divided by 5 years to derive an average annual cost for the first 5-year period.

Table 11—Annual net benefits (dollars per tree) at 5-year intervals and 40-year average for a representative medium tree (Norway maple)

Total net benefits	Year 5	Year 10	Year 15	Year 20	Year 25	Year 30	Year 35	Year 40	40-year average
					Dollars				
Yard: west	-5	36	46	53	57	56	57	57	45
Yard: south	-9	26	29	34	37	35	37	38	29
Yard: east	-8	30	36	42	46	44	45	46	35
Public	-8	26	31	36	39	37	38	39	30

Note: Annual values incorporate effects of tree loss. We assume that 13 percent of trees planted die during the first 5 years and 30.1 percent during the remaining 35 years for a total mortality of 43.1 percent. See table 9 for annual benefits and table 10 for annual costs.

Table 12—Annual benefits (dollars per tree) at 5-year intervals and 40-year average for a representative large tree (white ash)

Benefits/tree	Year 5		Year 10		Year 15		Year 20		Year 25		Year 30		Year 35		Year 40		40-year average	
	RU	Value	RU	Value	RU	Value	RU	Value	RU	Value	RU	Value	RU	Value	RU	Value	RU	Value
		Dollars		Dollars		Dollars		Dollars		Dollars		Dollars		Dollars		Dollars		Dollars
Cooling (kWh):																		
Yard: west	48	3.90	176	14.42	306	25.10	395	32.42	459	37.63	495	40.55	515	42.20	522	42.83	364	29.88
Yard: south	22	1.81	91	7.43	167	13.69	247	20.25	305	25.03	355	29.08	388	31.80	409	33.54	248	20.33
Yard: east	28	2.32	113	9.23	203	16.62	281	23.01	337	27.63	377	30.87	402	32.93	416	34.11	269	22.09
Public	21	1.71	81	6.65	145	11.85	209	17.13	256	20.96	296	24.27	323	26.49	342	28.06	209	17.14
Heating (therms):																		
Yard: west	1.43	1.67	4.81	5.61	7.66	8.93	9.17	10.69	10.21	11.91	10.31	12.03	10.23	11.93	9.82	11.45	7.95	9.28
Yard: south	0.71	0.83	1.98	2.32	2.67	3.12	3.28	3.83	3.71	4.33	3.82	4.46	3.85	4.49	3.72	4.35	2.97	3.47
Yard: east	1.06	1.24	3.66	4.27	5.87	6.84	7.38	8.61	8.45	9.86	8.76	10.21	8.85	10.33	8.64	10.08	6.58	7.68
Public	1.82	2.12	6.25	7.30	10.24	11.94	12.67	14.78	14.38	16.77	14.77	17.23	14.85	17.32	14.42	16.83	11.17	13.04
Net energy (kWh):																		
Yard: west	90	5.58	317	20.03	531	34.04	664	43.12	758	49.54	797	52.58	814	54.14	810	54.29	598	39.16
Yard: south	43	2.65	149	9.74	245	16.81	343	24.08	414	29.36	467	33.54	501	36.29	518	37.88	335	23.79
Yard: east	59	3.56	220	13.49	375	23.46	497	31.62	585	37.49	633	41.09	661	43.26	669	44.18	462	29.77
Public	74	3.83	264	13.94	445	23.80	580	31.91	677	37.73	729	41.51	758	43.81	765	44.88	537	30.18
Net carbon dioxide (lb):																		
Yard: west	58	0.19	208	0.70	359	1.20	466	1.55	545	1.82	592	1.98	623	2.08	638	2.13	436	1.46
Yard: south	30	0.10	112	0.37	196	0.66	286	0.95	354	1.18	411	1.37	453	1.51	482	1.61	290	0.97
Yard: east	39	0.13	148	0.49	260	0.87	359	1.20	433	1.45	485	1.62	522	1.74	545	1.82	349	1.17
Public	42	0.14	155	0.52	269	0.90	368	1.23	442	1.48	496	1.66	534	1.78	558	1.86	358	1.20
Air pollution (lb)[a]:																		
Ozone uptake	0.052	0.03	0.219	0.11	0.410	0.21	0.622	0.32	0.805	0.41	0.991	0.51	1.155	0.59	1.317	0.67	0.70	0.36
Nitrogen dioxide uptake + avoided	0.077	0.04	0.294	0.15	0.519	0.26	0.712	0.36	0.854	0.44	0.958	0.49	1.029	0.52	1.074	0.55	0.69	0.35
Sulfur dioxide uptake + avoided	0.152	0.01	0.588	0.04	1.049	0.06	1.447	0.09	1.735	0.10	1.946	0.12	2.080	0.12	2.160	0.13	1.39	0.08
Small particulate matter uptake + avoided	0.020	0.02	0.112	0.10	0.270	0.25	0.479	0.44	0.681	0.63	0.874	0.80	1.055	0.97	1.227	1.13	0.59	0.54
Volatile organic compounds avoided	0.014	0	0.052	0.01	0.092	0.01	0.127	0.02	0.152	0.02	0.170	0.02	0.181	0.03	0.188	0.03	0.12	0.02
Biogenic volatile organic compounds released	0	0	0	0	0	0	0	0	0	0	0	0	0	0	0	0	0	0
Total air pollution avoided + net uptake	0.315	0.10	1.266	0.41	2.340	0.80	3.387	1.23	4.227	1.60	4.938	1.94	5.500	2.23	5.966	2.50	3.49	1.35
Hydrology (gal)																		
Rainfall interception	82	0.41	349	1.75	654	3.27	993	4.96	1,285	6.43	1,582	7.91	1,843	9.22	2,102	10.51	1,111	5.56
Aesthetics and other:																		
Yard		11.45		32.79		40.55		39.37		33.51		25.47		16.68		10.19		26.25
Public		12.79		36.62		45.29		43.98		37.43		28.44		18.63		11.38		29.32
Total benefits:																		
Yard: west		17.72		55.67		79.85		90.24		92.90		89.87		84.35		79.62		73.78
Yard: south		14.70		45.05		62.08		70.60		72.08		70.22		65.93		62.70		57.92
Yard: east		15.65		48.93		68.95		78.39		80.47		78.02		73.14		69.21		64.09
Public		17.26		53.24		74.05		83.30		84.67		81.45		75.68		71.14		67.60

Note: Annual values incorporate effects of tree loss. We assume that 13 percent of trees planted die during the first 5 years and 30.1 percent during the remaining 35 years for a total mortality of 43.1 percent. RU = resource unit.

[a] Values are the same for yard and public trees.

Table 13—Annual costs (dollars per tree) at 5-year intervals and 40-year average for a representative large tree (white ash)

Costs	Year 5	Year 10	Year 15	Year 20	Year 25	Year 30	Year 35	Year 40	40-year average
					Dollars				
Tree and planting[a]:									
Yard	35.00								4.38
Public	28.00								3.50
Pruning:									
Yard	0.23	2.45	2.37	2.30	6.34	6.13	5.91	5.70	3.92
Public	5.44	6.20	5.88	5.56	8.73	8.20	7.66	7.12	6.97
Remove and dispose:									
Yard	0.08	1.14	1.78	2.37	2.92	3.43	3.91	4.37	2.31
Public	0.26	1.36	2.12	2.83	3.48	4.09	4.66	5.20	2.77
Pest and disease									
Yard	0.04	0.10	0.15	0.19	0.22	0.25	0.28	0.30	0.18
Public	0.04	0.09	0.13	0.16	0.18	0.20	0.22	0.22	0.14
Infrastructure repair:									
Yard	0.06	0.13	0.20	0.26	0.31	0.35	0.39	0.42	0.24
Public	0.41	0.95	1.41	1.77	2.06	2.27	2.42	2.51	1.60
Irrigation:									
Yard	0	0	0	0	0	0	0	0	0
Public	1.34	0	0	0	0	0	0	0	0.18
Cleanup:									
Yard	0.02	0.04	0.06	0.08	0.09	0.10	0.11	0.12	0.07
Public	0.12	0.28	0.41	0.52	0.60	0.66	0.70	0.73	0.47
Liability and legal:									
Yard	0	0	0.01	0.01	0.01	0.01	0.01	0.01	0.01
Public	0.01	0.03	0.04	0.06	0.06	0.07	0.08	0.08	0.05
Admin. and other:									
Yard	0	0	0	0	0	0	0	0	0
Public	0.81	1.87	2.76	3.48	4.03	4.45	4.74	4.92	3.14
Total costs:									
Yard	35.43	3.86	4.57	5.20	9.90	10.28	10.62	10.92	11.11
Public	36.43	10.78	12.76	14.37	19.15	19.94	20.47	20.79	18.81

Note: Annual values incorporate effects of tree loss. We assume that 13 percent of trees planted die during the first 5 years and 30.1 percent during the remaining 35 years for a total mortality of 43.1 percent.

[a]Although tree and planting costs occur in year 1, this value was divided by 5 years to derive an average annual cost for the first 5-year period.

Table 14—Annual net benefits (dollars per tree) at 5-year intervals and 40-year average for a representative large tree (white ash)

Total net benefits	Year 5	Year 10	Year 15	Year 20	Year 25	Year 30	Year 35	Year 40	40-year average
					Dollars				
Yard: west	-18	52	75	85	83	80	74	69	63
Yard: south	-21	41	58	65	62	60	55	52	47
Yard: east	-20	45	64	73	71	68	63	58	53
Public	-19	42	61	69	66	62	55	50	49

Note: Annual values incorporate effects of tree loss. We assume that 13 percent of trees planted die during the first 5 years and 30.1 percent during the remaining 35 years for a total mortality of 43.1 percent. See table 12 for annual benefits and table 13 for annual costs.

Table 15—Annual benefits (dollars per tree) at 5-year intervals and 40-year average for a representative conifer tree (blue spruce)

Benefits/tree	Year 5		Year 10		Year 15		Year 20		Year 25		Year 30		Year 35		Year 40		40-year average	
	RU	Value	RU	Value	RU	Value	RU	Value	RU	Value	RU	Value	RU	Value	RU	Value	RU	Value
		Dollars		*Dollars*		*Dollars*		*Dollars*		*Dollars*		*Dollars*		*Dollars*		*Dollars*		*Dollars*
Cooling (kWh):																		
Yard	17	1.39	40	3.28	57	4.67	71	5.82	80	6.56	87	7.13	90	7.38	91	7.46	67	5.46
Public	17	1.39	40	3.28	57	4.67	71	5.82	80	6.56	87	7.13	90	7.38	91	7.46	67	5.46
Heating (therms):																		
Yard	2.57	3.00	4.99	5.82	6.60	7.70	7.69	8.97	8.28	9.67	8.75	10.21	8.77	10.23	8.71	10.16	7.05	8.22
Public	2.57	3.00	4.99	5.82	6.60	7.70	7.69	8.97	8.28	9.67	8.75	10.21	8.77	10.23	8.71	10.16	7.05	8.22
Net energy (kWh):																		
Yard	92	4.39	186	9.10	250	12.37	297	14.79	323	16.22	344	17.34	347	17.61	346	17.62	273	13.68
Public	92	4.39	186	9.10	250	12.37	297	14.79	323	16.22	344	17.34	347	17.61	346	17.62	273	13.68
Net carbon dioxide (lb):																		
Yard	46	0.15	97	0.32	134	0.45	161	0.54	178	0.59	191	0.64	194	0.65	195	0.65	150	0.50
Public	46	0.15	97	0.32	134	0.45	161	0.54	178	0.59	191	0.64	194	0.65	195	0.65	150	0.50
Air pollution (lb)[a]																		
Ozone uptake	0.042	0.02	0.108	0.06	0.161	0.08	0.213	0.11	0.252	0.13	0.292	0.15	0.322	0.16	0.352	0.18	0.22	0.11
Nitrogen dioxide uptake + avoided	0.064	0.03	0.142	0.07	0.197	0.10	0.243	0.12	0.271	0.14	0.294	0.15	0.303	0.15	0.308	0.16	0.23	0.12
Sulfur dioxide uptake + avoided	0.087	0.01	0.204	0.01	0.290	0.02	0.365	0.02	0.410	0.02	0.447	0.03	0.460	0.03	0.467	0.03	0.34	0.02
Small particulate matter uptake + avoided	0.014	0.01	0.050	0.05	0.101	0.09	0.163	0.15	0.218	0.20	0.268	0.25	0.269	0.25	0.270	0.25	0.17	0.16
Volatile organic compounds avoided	0.009	0.00	0.020	0.00	0.028	0.00	0.035	0.00	0.039	0.01	0.043	0.01	0.044	0.01	0.044	0.01	0.03	0.01
Biogenic volatile organic compounds released	-0.057	-0.01	-0.223	-0.03	-0.601	-0.08	-1.344	-0.19	-2.363	-0.33	-3.656	-0.51	-3.656	-0.51	-3.656	-0.51	-1.94	-0.27
Total air pollution avoided + net uptake	0.159	0.06	0.301	0.16	0.176	0.21	-0.325	0.21	-1.173	0.17	-2.312	0.08	-2.258	0.09	-2.215	0.12	-0.96	0.14
Hydrology (gal)																		
Rainfall interception	262	1.31	671	3.36	1,014	5.07	1,390	6.95	1,681	8.41	1,972	9.86	2,218	11.09	2,463	12.32	1,459	7.30
Aesthetics and other:																		
Yard		10.63		11.52		11.55		11.12		10.51		9.82		9.11		8.39		10.33
Public		11.87		12.87		12.90		12.42		11.74		10.97		10.18		9.37		11.54
Total benefits:																		
Yard		16.54		24.46		29.65		33.61		35.90		37.74		38.55		39.10		31.95
Public		17.78		25.81		31.00		34.91		37.13		38.89		39.62		40.08		33.15

Note: Annual values incorporate effects of tree loss. We assume that 13 percent of trees planted die during the first 5 years and 30.1 percent during the remaining 35 years for a total mortality of 43.1 percent. RU = resource unit.

[a] Values are the same for yard and public trees.

Table 16—Annual costs (dollars per tree) at 5-year intervals and 40-year average for a representative conifer tree (blue spruce)

Costs	Year 5	Year 10	Year 15	Year 20	Year 25	Year 30	Year 35	Year 40	40-year average
				Dollars					
Tree and planting[a]:									
Yard	35.00								4.38
Public	28.00								3.50
Pruning:									
Yard	0.02	0.02	0.24	0.23	0.22	0.21	0.21	0.57	0.17
Public	0.54	0.33	0.59	0.56	0.52	0.49	0.46	0.71	0.50
Remove and dispose:									
Yard	0.87	1.24	1.75	2.19	2.57	2.92	3.23	3.52	2.07
Public	2.24	1.48	2.09	2.61	3.07	3.48	3.85	4.19	2.51
Pest and disease									
Yard	0.05	0.10	0.14	0.17	0.20	0.22	0.23	0.24	0.16
Public	0.05	0.09	0.12	0.15	0.16	0.17	0.18	0.18	0.13
Infrastructure repair:									
Yard	0.07	0.15	0.20	0.24	0.27	0.30	0.32	0.34	0.22
Public	0.54	1.03	1.38	1.64	1.81	1.93	1.99	2.02	1.45
Irrigation:									
Yard	0	0	0	0	0	0	0	0	0
Public	1.34	0	0	0	0	0	0	0	0.18
Cleanup:									
Yard	0.02	0.04	0.06	0.07	0.08	0.09	0.09	0.10	0.06
Public	0.16	0.30	0.40	0.48	0.53	0.56	0.58	0.59	0.42
Liability and legal:									
Yard	0	0	0.01	0.01	0.01	0.01	0.01	0.01	0.01
Public	0.02	0.03	0.04	0.05	0.06	0.06	0.06	0.06	0.05
Admin./inspect/other:									
Yard	0	0	0	0	0	0	0	0	0
Public	1.07	1.07	2.72	3.21	3.55	3.78	3.91	3.96	2.84
Total costs:									
Yard	36.04	1.55	2.40	2.91	3.36	3.75	4.09	4.77	7.07
Public	33.96	4.33	7.35	8.68	9.70	10.47	11.04	11.72	11.57

Note: Annual values incorporate effects of tree loss. We assume that 13 percent of trees planted die during the first 5 years and 30.1 percent during the remaining 35 years for a total mortality of 43.1 percent. RU = resource unit.

[a] Although tree and planting costs occur in year 1, this value was divided by 5 years to derive an average annual cost for the first 5-year period.

Table 17—Annual net benefits (dollars per tree) at 5-year intervals and 40-year average for a representative conifer tree (blue spruce)

Total net benefits	Year 5	Year 10	Year 15	Year 20	Year 25	Year 30	Year 35	Year 40	40-year average
				Dollars					
Yard	-19	23	27	31	33	34	34	34	25
Public	-16	21	24	26	27	28	29	28	22

Note: Annual values incorporate effects of tree loss. We assume that 13 percent of trees planted die during the first 5 years and 30.1 percent during the remaining 35 years for a total mortality of 43.1 percent. See table 15 for annual benefits and table 16 for annual costs.

Appendix 3: Procedures for Estimating Benefits and Costs

Approach

Pricing Benefits and Costs

In this study, annual benefits and costs over a 40-year planning horizon were estimated for newly planted trees in three residential yard locations (east, south, and west of the dwelling unit) and a public streetside or park location. Trees in these hypothetical locations are called "yard" and "public" trees, respectively. Prices were assigned to each cost (e.g., planting, pruning, removal, irrigation, infrastructure repair, liability) and benefit (e.g., heating/cooling, energy savings, air-pollution reduction, stormwater-runoff reduction) through direct estimation and implied valuation of benefits as environmental externalities. This approach made it possible to estimate the net benefits of plantings in "typical" locations with "typical" tree species.

To account for differences in the mature size and growth rates of different tree species, we report results for a small (crabapple), medium (Norway maple), and large (white ash) deciduous tree and for a conifer (blue spruce) (see "Common and Scientific Names" section). Results are reported for 5-year intervals for 40 years.

Mature tree height is frequently used to characterize small, medium, and large species because matching tree height to available overhead space is an important design consideration. However, in this analysis, leaf surface area (LSA) and crown diameter were also used to characterize **mature tree size**. These additional measurements are useful indicators for many functional benefits of trees that relate to leaf-atmosphere processes (e.g., interception, transpiration, photosynthesis). Tree growth rates, dimensions, and LSA estimates are based on tree growth modeling.

Growth Modeling

Growth models are based on data collected in Boise, Idaho. The city's Parks and Recreation Department provided an inventory of Boise's municipal trees that included 23,262 trees.

Tree-growth models developed from Boise data were used as the basis for modeling tree growth for this report. Using Boise's tree inventory, we measured a stratified random sample of 20 of the most common tree species to establish relations between tree age, size, leaf area, and biomass. The species were as follows:

- Norway maple (*Acer platanoides*)

- Silver maple (*Acer saccharinum*)

- Sugar maple (*Acer saccharum*)

- Northern catalpa (*Catalpa speciosa*)

- Hawthorn (*Crataegus* sp.)

- White ash (*Fraxinus americana*)

- Green ash (*Fraxinus pennsylvanica*)

- Honeylocust (*Gleditsia triacanthos*)

- Black walnut (*Juglans nigra*)

- Sweetgum (*Liquidambar styraciflua*)

- Crabapple (*Malus* sp.)

- Blue spruce (*Picea pungens*)

- Scotch pine (*Pinus sylvestris*)

- London planetree (*Platanus hybrida*)

- American sycamore (*Platanus occidentalis*)

- Callery pear (*Pyrus calleryana*)

- Northern red oak (*Quercus rubra*)

- Black locust (*Robinia pseudoacacia*)

- American linden (*Tilia americana*)

- Siberian elm (*Ulmus pumila*)

For the growth models, information spanning the life cycle of predominant tree species was collected. The inventory was stratified into the following nine diameter-at-breast-height (d.b.h.) classes:

- 0 to 2.9 in

- 3.0 to 5.9 in

- 6.0 to 11.9 in

- 12.0 to 17.9 in

- 18.0 to 23.9 in

- 24.0 to 29.9 in

- 30.0 to 35.9 in

- 36.0 to 41.9 in

- ≥ 42.0 in

Thirty to sixty trees of each species were randomly selected for surveying, along with an equal number of alternative trees. Tree measurements included d.b.h. (to nearest 0.1 cm [0.04 in] by sonar measuring device), tree crown height, and bole height (to nearest 0.5 m [1.6 ft] by clinometer), crown diameter in two directions (parallel and perpendicular to nearest street to nearest 0.5 m [1.6 ft] by sonar measuring device), tree condition, and location. Replacement trees were sampled when trees from the original sample population could not be located. Tree age was determined by street-tree managers. Fieldwork was conducted in August and September 2005.

Crown volume and leaf area were estimated from computer processing of tree-crown images obtained with a digital camera. The method has shown greater accuracy than other techniques (± 20 percent of actual leaf area) in estimating crown volume and leaf area of open-grown trees (Peper and McPherson 2003).

Linear regression was used to fit predictive models with d.b.h. as a function of age for each of the 20 sampled species. Predictions of LSA, crown diameter, and height metrics were modeled as a function of d.b.h. by using best-fit models. After inspecting the growth curves for each species, we selected the typical small, medium, and large tree species for this report.

Reporting Results

Results are reported in terms of annual values per tree planted. However, to make these calculations realistic, mortality rates are included. Based on our survey of regional municipal foresters and commercial arborists, this analysis assumed that 43 percent of the hypothetical planted trees died over the 40-year period. Annual mortality rates were 2.6 percent for the first 5 years, and 0.85 percent per year after that. The accounting approach "grows" trees in different locations and uses computer simulation to directly calculate the annual flow of benefits and costs as trees mature and die (McPherson 1992).

Benefits and costs are directly connected with tree-size variables such as trunk d.b.h., tree canopy cover, and LSA. For instance, pruning and removal costs usually increase with tree size, expressed as d.b.h. For some parameters, such as sidewalk repair, costs are negligible for young trees but increase relatively rapidly as tree roots grow large enough to heave pavement. For other parameters, such as air-pollutant uptake and rainfall interception, benefits are related to tree canopy cover and leaf area.

Most benefits occur on an annual basis, but some costs are periodic. For instance, street trees may be pruned on regular cycles but are removed in a less regular fashion (e.g., when they pose a hazard or soon after they die). In this analysis, most costs and benefits are reported for the year in which they occur. However, periodic costs such as pruning, pest and disease control, and infrastructure repair are presented on an average annual basis. Although spreading one-time costs over each year of a maintenance cycle does not alter the 40-year nominal expenditure, it can lead to inaccuracies if future costs are discounted to the present.

Benefit and Cost Valuation

Source of cost estimates—

Frequency and costs of tree management were estimated based on surveys with municipal foresters from Boise, Lewiston, Nampa, Payette, and Caldwell, Idaho, and Carson City, Nevada. Several arborists from Boise and Meridian, Idaho, provided information on tree management costs on residential properties.

Monetizing benefits—

To monetize effects of trees on energy use, we take the perspective of a residential customer by using retail electricity and natural-gas prices for utilities serving the Temperate Interior West, including Boise, Reno, Nevada, and Yakima, Washington. The retail price of energy reflects a full accounting of costs as paid by the end user, such as the utility costs of power generation, transmission, distribution, administration, marketing, and profit. This perspective aligns with our modeling method, which calculates energy effects of trees based on differences among consumers in heating and air conditioning equipment types, saturations, building construction types, and base loads.

The preferred way to value air quality benefits from trees is to first determine the costs of damages to human health from polluted air, then calculate the value of avoided costs because trees are cleaning the air. Economic valuation of damages to human health usually uses information on willingness to pay to avoid damages obtained via interviews or direct estimates of the monetary costs of damages (e.g., alleviating headaches, extending life). Empirical correlations developed by Wang and Santini (1995) reviewed 5 studies and 15 sets of regional cost data to relate per-ton costs of various pollutant emissions to regional ambient air quality measurements and population size. We use their damage-based estimates unless the values are negative, in which case we use their control-cost-based estimates.

Calculating Benefits

Calculating Energy Benefits

The prototypical building used as a basis for the simulations was typical of post-1980 construction practices and represents approximately one-third of the total single-family residential housing stock in the Temperate Interior West region. The house was a one-story, wood-frame, slab-on-grade building with a conditioned floor area of 2,070 ft^2, window area (double-glazed) of 263 ft^2, and wall and ceiling insulation of R13 and R31, respectively. The central cooling system had a **seasonal energy efficiency ratio** (SEER) of 10, and the natural-gas furnace had an **annual fuel utilization efficiency** (AFUE) of 78 percent. Building footprints were square, reflecting average impacts for a large number of buildings (McPherson and Simpson 1999). Buildings were simulated with 1.5-ft overhangs. Blinds had a visual density of 37 percent and were assumed to be closed when the air conditioner was operating. Summer thermostat settings were 78 °F; winter settings were 68 °F during the day and 60 °F at night. Because the prototype building was larger, but more energy efficient, than most other construction types, our projected energy savings can be considered similar to those for older, less thermally efficient, but smaller buildings. The energy simulations relied on typical meteorological data from Boise (Marion and Urban 1995).

Calculating energy savings—
The dollar value of energy savings was based on regional average residential electricity and natural-gas prices of $0.082/**kWh** and $1.17/**therm** (Idaho Power Company 2006, Intermountain Gas Company 2006). Homes were assumed to have central air conditioning and natural-gas heating.

Calculating shade effects—
Residential yard trees were within 60 ft of homes so as to directly shade walls and windows. Shade effects of these trees on building energy use were simulated for small, medium, and large trees at three tree-to-building distances, following methods outlined by McPherson and Simpson (1999). Results of shade effects for each tree were averaged over distance and weighted by occurrence within each of three distance classes: 28 percent at 10 to 20 ft (3 to 6 m), 68 percent at 20 to 40 ft (6 to 12 m), and 4 percent at 40 to 60 ft (12 to 18 m) (McPherson and Simpson 1999).

The small tree (crabapple) had visual densities of 85 percent during summer and 15 percent during winter, the medium tree (Norway maple) had visual densities of 69 percent during summer and 12 percent during winter, and the large tree (white ash) had visual densities of 78 percent during summer and 17 percent during winter. The conifer (blue spruce) had a visual density of 20 percent.

Leaf-off values for use in calculating winter shade were based on published values where available (Hammond et al. 1980, McPherson 1984). Foliation periods for deciduous trees were obtained from the literature (Hammond et al. 1980, McPherson 1984) and adjusted for Boise based on consultation with the city forester (Jorgenson 2006). The foliation periods of the trees were as follows: small tree 21 May–14 November, medium tree 21 May–7 November, large tree 21 May–20 October.

Results are reported for trees shading east-, south-, and west-facing surfaces. Our results for public trees are conservative in that we assumed that they do not provide shading benefits. For example, in Modesto, California, 15 percent of total annual dollar energy savings from street trees was due to shade and 85 percent due to **climate effects** (McPherson et al. 1999a).

Calculating climate effects—

In addition to localized shade effects, which were assumed to accrue only to residential yard trees, lowered air temperatures and windspeeds from increased neighborhood tree cover (referred to as climate effects) produced a net decrease in demand for winter heating and summer cooling (reduced windspeeds by themselves may increase or decrease cooling demand, depending on the circumstances). Climate effects on energy use, air temperature, and windspeed, as a function of neighborhood canopy cover, were estimated from published values (McPherson and Simpson 1999). Existing tree canopy plus building cover was 26 percent based on estimates of urban tree cover for Idaho (Nowak and Crane 2002). Canopy cover was calculated to increase by 4.3 percent, 6.6 percent, 8.8 percent, and 3.0 percent for 20-year-old small, medium, and large deciduous and coniferous trees, respectively, based on an effective lot size (actual lot size plus a portion of adjacent street and other rights-of-way) of 10,000 ft^2, and one tree on average was assumed per lot. Climate effects were estimated by simulating effects of wind reductions and air-temperature reductions on energy use. Climate effects accrued for both public and yard trees.

Calculating windbreak effects—

Trees near buildings result in additional windspeed reductions beyond those from the aggregate effects of trees throughout the neighborhood. This leads to a small additional reduction in annual heating energy use of about 0.5 percent per tree for this region (McPherson and Simpson 1999). Yard and public conifer trees were assumed to be windbreaks, and therefore located where they did not increase heating loads by obstructing winter sun. Windbreak effects were not attributed to deciduous trees, as their crowns are leafless and above the ground, and therefore do not block winds near ground level.

Atmospheric Carbon Dioxide Reduction

Calculating reduction in CO_2 emissions from power plants—

Conserving energy in buildings can reduce carbon dioxide (CO_2) emissions from power plants. Emission reductions were calculated as the product of energy savings for heating and cooling with CO_2 **emission factors** (table 18) based on data for Idaho Power Company, the local utility company in Boise, where the average fuel mix consists almost entirely of hydroelectric (99.9 percent) power (U.S. EPA 2003).

Table 18—Emissions factors and implied values for carbon dioxide and criteria air pollutants

Emission factor	Electricity[a]	Natural gas[b]	Implied value[c]
	Pounds per megawatt hour	*Pounds per therm*	*Dollars per pound*
Carbon dioxide	746	11.8	0.00334
Nitrogen dioxide	1.443	0.01020	0.51
Sulfur dioxide	0.988	0.00006	0.06
Small particulate matter	0.500	0.00075	0.92
Volatile organic compounds	0.460	0.00054	0.14

[a] U.S. EPA 2003, except Ottinger et al. 1990 for volatile organic compounds.

[b] U.S. EPA 1998.

[c] Carbon dioxide from Pearce 2003. Value for others based on methods of Wang and Santini (1995) using emissions concentrations from U.S. Environmental Protection Agency (2003) and population estimates from the U.S. Census Bureau (2006).

The value of \$6.68 per ton CO_2 reduction (table 18) was based on the average value given by Pearce (2003).

Calculating carbon storage—

Sequestration, the net rate of CO_2 storage in above- and belowground biomass over the course of one growing season, was calculated from tree height and d.b.h. data with biomass equations (Pillsbury et al. 1998). Volume estimates were converted to green- and dry-weight estimates (Markwardt 1930) and divided by 78 percent to incorporate root biomass. Dry-weight biomass was converted to carbon (50 percent) and these values were converted to CO_2. The amount of CO_2 sequestered each year is the annual increment of CO_2 stored as trees increase their biomass.

Calculating CO_2 released by power equipment—

Tree-related emissions of CO_2, based on gasoline and diesel fuel consumption during tree care in our survey cities, were calculated by using the value 0.89 lbs of CO_2 per in d.b.h. (Jorgenson 2006). This amount may overestimate CO_2 release associated with less intensively maintained residential yard trees.

Calculating CO_2 released during decomposition—

To calculate CO_2 released through decomposition of dead woody biomass, we conservatively estimated that dead trees were removed and mulched in the year that death occurred, and that 80 percent of their stored carbon was released to the atmosphere as CO_2 in the same year (McPherson and Simpson 1999).

Calculating reduction in air pollutant emissions—

Reductions in building energy use also result in reduced emission of air pollutants from power plants and space-heating equipment. Volatile organic hydrocarbons (VOCs) and nitrogen dioxide (NO_2)—both precursors of ozone formation—as well as sulfur dioxide (SO_2) and particulate matter <10 microns in diameter (PM_{10}) were considered. Changes in average annual emissions and their monetary values were calculated in the same way as for CO_2, with utility-specific emissions factors for electricity and heating fuels (Ottinger et al. 1990, U.S. EPA 1998). The price of emissions savings was derived from models that calculate the marginal cost of controlling different pollutants to meet air quality standards (Wang and Santini 1995). Emissions concentrations were obtained from U.S. EPA (2003) (table 18), and population estimates from the U.S. Census Bureau (2006).

Calculating pollutant uptake by trees—
Trees also remove pollutants from the atmosphere. The modeling method we applied was developed by Scott et al. (1998). It calculates hourly pollutant dry deposition per tree expressed as the product of deposition velocity ($V_d = 1/[R_a + R_b + R_c]$), pollutant concentration (*C*), canopy-projection area (*CP*), and a time step, where R_a, R_b and R_c are aerodynamic, boundary layer, and stomatal resistances. Hourly deposition velocities for each pollutant were calculated during the growing season by using estimates for the resistances ($R_a + R_b + R_c$) for each hour throughout the year. Hourly concentrations for O_3 and PM_{10} for Boise and NO_2 for Mountain Home, Idaho, were obtained from the Environmental Protection Agency (U.S. EPA 2006), and hourly meteorological data (i.e., air temperature, windspeed, solar radiation) were obtained from the Pacific Northwest Cooperative Agricultural Weather Network (Agrimet 2006). The year 2003 was chosen because it most closely approximated long-term, regional climate records. To set a value for pollutant uptake by trees, we used the procedure described above for emissions reductions (table 18). The monetary value for NO_2 was used for ozone.

Estimating BVOC emissions from trees—
Annual emissions for biogenic volatile organic compounds (BVOCs) were estimated for the four tree species by using the algorithms of Guenther et al. (1991, 1993). Annual emissions were simulated during the growing season over 40 years. The emission of carbon as isoprene was expressed as a product of the base emission rate (µg C per g dry foliar biomass per h), adjusted for sunlight and temperature and the amount of dry, foliar biomass present in the tree. Monoterpene emissions were estimated by using a base emission rate adjusted for temperature. The base emission rates for the four species were based on values reported in the literature (Benjamin and Winer 1998). Hourly emissions were summed to get monthly and annual emissions.

Annual dry foliar biomass was derived from field data collected in Boise, Idaho, during the late summer of 2005. The amount of foliar biomass present for each year of the simulated tree's life was unique for each species. Hourly air temperature and solar radiation data for 2003 described in the pollutant uptake section were used as model inputs.

Calculating net air quality benefits—

Net air quality benefits were calculated by subtracting the costs associated with BVOC emissions from benefits associated with pollutant uptake and avoided power plant emissions. The ozone-reduction benefit from lowering summertime air temperatures, thereby reducing hydrocarbon emissions from **anthropogenic** and biogenic sources, was estimated as a function of canopy cover following McPherson and Simpson (1999). They used peak summer air temperature reductions of 0.4 °F for each percentage increase in canopy cover. Hourly changes in air temperature were calculated by reducing this peak air temperature at every hour based on hourly maximum and minimum temperature for that day, scaled by magnitude of maximum total global solar radiation for each day relative to the maximum value for the year.

Stormwater Benefits

Estimating rainfall interception by tree canopies—

A numerical simulation model was used to estimate annual rainfall interception (Xiao et al. 2000). The interception model accounted for water intercepted by the tree, as well as throughfall and **stem flow**. Intercepted water is stored temporarily on canopy leaf and bark surfaces. Rainwater evaporates or drips from leaf surfaces and flows down the stem surface to the ground. Tree-canopy parameters that affect interception include species, leaf and stem surface areas, **shade coefficients** (visual density of the crown), foliation periods, and tree dimensions (e.g., tree height, crown height, crown diameter, and d.b.h.). Tree-height data were used to estimate windspeed at different heights above the ground and resulting rates of evaporation.

The volume of water stored in the tree crown was calculated from crown-projection area (area under tree dripline), **leaf area indices** (LAI, the ratio of LSA to crown projection area), and the depth of water captured by the canopy surface. Gap fractions, foliation periods, and tree surface saturation storage capacity influence the amount of projected throughfall. Tree surface saturation was 1.0 mm (0.04 in) for all trees.

Hourly meteorological and rainfall data for 2004 at the AgriMet Station (BOII) (The Pacific Northwest Cooperative Agricultural Weather Network, station's latitude 43° 36' 01" N, longitude 116° 10' 37" W, elevation 2,720 feet) in Boise,

Idaho, were used in this simulation. The year 2004 was chosen because, although the overall amount of rainfall was higher, it most closely approximated the monthly distribution of the long-term average rainfall. Annual precipitation at BOII during 2004 was 16.4 in. Storm events less than 0.1 in were assumed not to produce runoff and were dropped from the analysis. More complete descriptions of the interception model can be found in Xiao et al. (1998, 2000).

Calculating water quality protection and flood control benefit—
The benefits that result from reduced peak runoff include reduced property damage from flooding and reduced loss of soil and habitat from erosion and sediment flow. Reduced runoff also results in improved water quality in streams, lakes, and rivers. This can translate into improved aquatic habitats, less human illness owing to contact with contaminated water and reduced stormwater treatment costs.

According to Johanna Bell (2006), Boise spends approximately $1.97 million annually on operations, maintenance, and improvements to its stormwater management system (Bell 2006). To calculate annual runoff we assigned curve numbers for each land use (USDA SCS 1986). Land use percentages were obtained from the city geographic information system database (Wing 2006). We calculated runoff depth for each land use and found the citywide total to be 1,138 acre-feet. Given Boise's area of 68.1 mi^2 (176.4 km^2), the total annual runoff was 419.9 million gal. The annual stormwater control cost ($1.97 million/419.9 million gal) was estimated to be $0.005 per gallon of runoff.

Aesthetic and Other Benefits

Many benefits attributed to urban trees are difficult to translate into economic terms. Beautification, privacy, wildlife habitat, shade that increases human comfort, sense of place and well-being are services that are difficult to price. However, the value of some of these benefits may be captured in the property values of the land on which trees stand.

To estimate the value of these "other" benefits, we applied results of research that compared differences in sales prices of houses to statistically quantify the difference associated with trees. All else being equal, the difference in sales price reflects the willingness of buyers to pay for the benefits and costs associated with trees. This approach has the virtue of capturing in the sales price both the benefits and costs of trees as perceived by the buyers. Limitations to this approach include difficulty determining the value of individual trees on a property, the need to extrapolate results from studies done years ago, and the need to extrapolate results from front-yard trees on residential properties to trees in other locations (e.g., back yards, streets, parks, and nonresidential land).

Anderson and Cordell (1988) surveyed 844 single-family residences in Athens, Georgia, and found that each large front-yard tree was associated with a 0.88-percent increase in the average home sales price. This percentage of sales price was used as an indicator of the additional value a resident in the Temperate Interior West region would gain from selling a home with a large tree.

We used the average median home price for Boise ($155,500) as our starting point. Therefore, the value of a large tree that added 0.88 percent to the sales price of such a home was $1,322. To estimate annual benefits, the total added value was divided by the LSA of a 30-year-old white ash ($1,322 per 5,179 ft^2) to yield the base value of LSA, $0.255 per ft^2. This value was multiplied by the amount of leaf surface area added to the tree during 1 year of growth.

Additionally, not all street trees are as effective as front-yard trees in increasing property values. For example, trees adjacent to multifamily housing units will not increase the property value at the same rate as trees in front of single-family homes. Therefore, a citywide street tree reduction factor (0.93) was applied to prorate trees' value based on the assumption that trees adjacent to different land uses make different contributions to property sales prices. For this analysis, the street reduction factor reflects the distribution of street trees in Boise by land use. Reduction factors were single-home residential (100 percent), multihome residential (70 percent), small commercial (66 percent), industrial/institutional/large commercial (40 percent), park/vacant/other (40 percent) (Gonzales 2004, McPherson 2001).

Calculating the aesthetic and other benefits of residential yard trees—
To calculate the base value for a large tree on private residential property we assumed that a 30-year-old white ash in the front yard increased the property sales price by $1,322. Approximately 75 percent of all yard trees, however, are in back yards (Richards et al. 1984). Lacking specific research findings, it was assumed that back-yard trees had 75 percent of the impact on "curb appeal" and sales price compared to front-yard trees. The average annual aesthetic and other benefits for a tree on private property were, therefore, estimated as $0.19 per ft^2 LSA. To estimate annual benefits, this value was multiplied by the amount of leaf surface area added to the tree during 1 year of growth.

Calculating the aesthetic value of a public tree—
The base value of street trees was calculated in the same way as yard trees. However, because street trees may be adjacent to land with little resale potential, an adjusted value was calculated. An analysis of street trees in Modesto, California, sampled from aerial photographs (sample size 8 percent of street trees), found that 15 percent were located adjacent to nonresidential or commercial property

(McPherson et al. 1999a). We assumed that 33 percent of these trees—or 5 percent of the entire street-tree population—produced no benefits associated with property value increases.

Although the impact of parks on real estate values has been reported (Hammer et al. 1974, Schroeder 1982, Tyrvainen 1999), to our knowledge, the onsite and external benefits of park trees alone have not been isolated (More et al. 1988). After reviewing the literature and recognizing an absence of data, we made the conservative estimate that park trees had half the impact on property prices of street trees.

Given these assumptions, typical large street and park trees were estimated to increase property values by \$0.24 and \$0.13 per ft^2 LSA, respectively. Assuming that 80 percent of all municipal trees were on streets and 20 percent in parks, a weighted average benefit of \$0.217/ft^2 LSA was calculated for each tree.

Calculating Costs

Tree management costs were estimated based on surveys with municipal foresters from Boise, Lewiston, Nampa, Payette, and Caldwell, Idaho, and Carson City, Nevada. In addition, several commercial arborists from Boise and Meridian, Idaho, provided information on tree management costs on residential properties.

Planting

Planting costs include the cost of the tree and the cost for planting, staking, and mulching the tree. Based on our survey of Temperate Interior West municipal and commercial arborists, planting costs ranged widely from \$65 for a 10-gal tree to \$350 for a 2-in tree. In this analysis we assumed that a 2-in yard tree was planted at a cost of \$175. The cost for planting a 1.5-in public tree was \$140.

Pruning

Pruning costs for public trees—
After studying data from municipal forestry programs and their contractors, we assumed that young public trees were inspected and pruned once every 4 years during the first 5 years after planting at a cost of \$25 per tree. After this training period, inspection and pruning occurred once every 10 years. Pruning for small trees (< 20 ft tall) cost \$40 per tree. More expensive equipment and more time was required to prune medium (\$75 per tree) and large trees (\$125 per tree). After factoring in pruning frequency, annualized costs were \$6.24, \$4, \$7.50, and \$12.50 per tree for public young, small, medium, and large trees, respectively. Conifers require pruning much less frequently; the average annualized cost was \$3.23.

Pruning costs for yard trees—

Based on findings from our survey of commercial arborists in the Temperate Interior West region, pruning cycles for yard trees were about the same as public trees, but only about 20 percent of all private trees were professionally pruned (**contract rate**), although the number of professionally pruned trees grows as the trees grow. We assumed that professionals are paid to prune all large trees, 60 percent of the medium trees, and only 6 percent of the small and young trees and conifers (Summit and McPherson 1998). Using these contract rates, along with average pruning prices ($40, $60, $175, and $300 for young, small, medium, and large trees, respectively), the average annual costs for pruning a yard tree were $0.24, $0.28, $2.63, and $7.50 for young, small, medium, and large trees, respectively. The annualized cost for pruning conifers was $0.16.

Tree and Stump Removal

The costs for tree removal and disposal were $20 per in d.b.h. for public trees, and $25 per in d.b.h. for yard trees. Stump removal costs were $7 per in d.b.h. for public trees and $9 per in d.b.h. for yard trees. Therefore, total costs for removal and disposal of trees and stumps were $27 per in d.b.h. for public trees, and $34 per in d.b.h. for yard trees. Removal costs of trees under 3 inches in diameter were $10 for yard and public trees.

Pest and Disease Control

Pest and disease control measures in the Temperate Interior West are minimal, with cities spending only about $0.16 per tree per year. Because of lack of data from the residential arborists surveys, we used the same value for yard trees.

Irrigation Costs

Costs for watering during the critical 5-year establishment period were estimated at $1.48 for public trees per tree per year, mainly for the labor costs involved in visiting the trees with a water truck or other time-intensive method. Beyond the establishment period, it is assumed that trees have been planted into irrigated landscapes and therefore the cost of additional water for the trees is negligible. No costs for irrigating yard trees were included because these were also assumed to be planted in irrigated landscapes where the cost of additional water is negligible and the additional labor involved for extra watering during the first 5 years by the resident was also considered negligible.

Other Costs for Public and Yard Trees

Other costs associated with the management of trees include expenditures for infrastructure repair/root pruning, leaf-litter cleanup, and inspection/administration.

Infrastructure conflict costs—

As trees and sidewalks age, roots can cause damage to sidewalks, curbs, paving, and sewer lines. Sidewalk repair is typically one of the largest expenses for public trees (McPherson and Peper 1995). Infrastructure-related expenditures for public trees in Temperate Interior West communities were approximately $2.23 per tree on an annual basis. Roots from most trees in yards do not damage sidewalks and sewers. Therefore, the cost for yard trees was estimated to be only 10 percent of the cost for public trees.

Litter and storm cleanup costs—

The average annual cost per tree for litter cleanup (i.e., street sweeping, storm-damage cleanup) was $0.65 per tree ($0.057 per in d.b.h.). This value was based on average annual litter cleanup costs and storm cleanup, assuming a large storm results in extraordinary costs about once a decade. Because most residential yard trees are not littering the streets with leaves, it was assumed that cleanup costs for yard trees were 10 percent of those for public trees.

Inspection and administration costs—

Municipal tree programs have administrative costs for salaries of supervisors and clerical staff, operating costs, and overhead. Our survey found that the average annual cost for inspection and administration associated with street- and park-tree management was $3.50 per tree ($0.384 per in d.b.h.). Trees on private property do not accrue this expense.

Calculating Net Benefits

Benefits Accrue at Different Scales

When calculating net benefits, it is important to recognize that trees produce benefits that accrue both on- and offsite. Benefits are realized at four scales: parcel, neighborhood, community, and global. For example, property owners with onsite trees not only benefit from increased property values, but they may also directly benefit from improved human health (e.g., reduced exposure to cancer-causing ultraviolet radiation) and greater psychological well-being through visual and direct contact with plants. However, on the cost side, increased health care costs owing to allergies and respiratory ailments related to pollen may be incurred because of nearby trees. We assume that these intangible benefits and costs are reflected in what we term "aesthetics and other benefits."

The property owner can obtain additional economic benefits from onsite trees depending on their location and condition. For example, carefully located onsite trees can provide air-conditioning savings by shading windows and walls and cooling building microclimates. This benefit can extend to adjacent neighbors who benefit from shade and air-temperature reductions that lower their cooling costs.

Neighborhood attractiveness and property values can be influenced by the extent of tree canopy cover on individual properties. At the community scale, benefits are realized through cleaner air and water, as well as social, educational, and employment and job training benefits that can reduce costs for health care, welfare, crime prevention, and other social service programs.

Reductions in atmospheric CO_2 concentrations owing to trees are an example of benefits that are realized at the global scale.

Annual benefits are calculated as:

$B = E + AQ + CO_2 + H + A$

where

E = value of net annual energy savings (cooling and heating)

AQ = value of annual air-quality improvement (pollutant uptake, avoided power plant emissions, and BVOC emissions)

CO_2 = value of annual CO_2 reductions (sequestration, avoided emissions, release from tree care and decomposition)

H = value of annual stormwater-runoff reductions

A = value of annual aesthetics and other benefits

On the other side of the benefit-cost equation are costs for tree planting and management. Expenditures are borne by property owners (irrigation, pruning, and removal) and the community (pollen and other health care costs). Annual costs (C) are the sum of costs for residential yard trees (C_Y) and public trees (C_P):

$C_Y = P + T + R + D + I + S + Cl + L$

$C_P = P + T + R + D + I + S + Cl + L + A$

where

P = cost of tree and planting

T = average annual tree pruning cost

R = annualized tree and stump removal and disposal cost

D = average annual pest- and disease-control cost

I = annual irrigation cost

S = average annual cost to repair/mitigate infrastructure damage

Cl = annual litter and storm cleanup cost

L = average annual cost for litigation and settlements from tree-related claims

A = annual program administration, inspection, and other costs

Net benefits are calculated as the difference between total benefits and costs:

Net benefits = $B - C$

Benefit-cost ratios (BCR) are calculated as the ratio of benefits to costs:

BCR = B / C

Limitations of This Study

This analysis does not account for the wide variety of trees planted in Temperate Interior West communities or their diverse placement. It does not incorporate the full range of climatic differences within the region that influence potential energy, air quality, and hydrology benefits. Estimating aesthetics and other benefits is difficult because the research in this area is not well developed. We considered only residential and municipal tree cost scenarios, but realize that the costs associated with planting and managing trees can differ widely depending on program characteristics. For example, our analysis does not incorporate costs incurred by utility companies and passed on to customers for maintenance of trees under power lines. However, as described by examples in chapter 3, local cost data can be substituted for the data in this report to evaluate the benefits and costs of alternative programs.

In this analysis, results are presented in terms of future values of benefits and costs, not present values. Thus, findings do not incorporate the time value of money or inflation. We assume that the user intends to invest in community forests and our objective is to identify the relative magnitudes of future costs and benefits. If the user is interested in comparing an investment in urban forestry with other investment opportunities, it is important to discount all future benefits and costs to the beginning of the investment period. For example, trees with a future value of $100,000 in 10 years have a present value of $55,840, assuming a 6 percent annual interest rate.

www.ingramcontent.com/pod-product-compliance
Lightning Source LLC
Chambersburg PA
CBHW080303290526
45790CB00005B/1917